NEW ENGLAND
RECORDS

NEW ENGLAND
RECORDS

Roy Bongartz

The Stephen Greene Press

BRATTLEBORO, VERMONT

The author wishes to thank the following institutions and individuals who have furnished photos for *New England Records*: Mystic Marinelife Aquarium, Mystic, Conn. (page 5); Claes Oldenburg, *Lipstick Ascending on Caterpillar Tracks,* Yale University Art Gallery, Gift of Colossal Keepsake Corporation, New Haven, Conn. (page 8); Sikorsky Aircraft (Division of United Technologies), Stratford, Conn. (page 14); Arthur D. Little, Inc., Cambridge, Mass. (page 22); Frank C. Usin, Windsor, Vt. (page 28); Maine State Development Office, Augusta, Me. (pages 30, 84); E. R. Landgraf, Moose River, Me. (page 33); Office of Public Information, Yale University (page 34); Massachusetts Department of Commerce and Development, Boston, Mass. (pages 46, 142); Connecticut Department of Commerce, Hartford, Conn. (pages 58, 115); News Bureau, University of Massachusetts, Amherst, Mass. (page 96); Vermont Historical Society, Montpelier, Vt. (page 99); Central Vermont Public Service Corporation, Rutland, Vt. (page 101); State of New Hampshire, photo by Dick Smith, North Conway, N.H. (page 132); News Office, Massachusetts Institute of Technology, Cambridge, Mass. (page 174).

This book has been produced
in the United States of America.
It is published by The Stephen Greene Press,
Brattleboro, Vermont 05301

LIBRARY OF CONGRESS CATALOGING IN PUBLICATION DATA
Bongartz, Roy.
   New England records.

   Includes index.
   1. New England—Miscellanea. 2. Curiosities and wonders. I. Title.
F4.5.B66   974′.04   78-4647
ISBN 0-8289-0330-1

Contents

Preface

The American mania for setting records, for doing things or having things in a big way—the tallest, the longest, the oldest, the most expensive—may reach its height in a Texas-style myth of enormousness and bestness, while we may prefer to suppose that New Englanders remain cooler, composed in the face of challenges to superlative greatnesses. This book shows, however, that the six New England states can take on the other forty-four, and the rest of the world combined, in any kind of records contest you might care to challenge them with.

New England does not have the world's oldest town (which is Jericho in Jordan, dating back some 7,500 years before New England existed) but it does have plenty of towns that are the world's—or America's—oldest *for something,* and that is what counts: Oldest town manufacturing modern scythe snathes, for instance (Sterling, Mass.), or oldest town to have its bank robbed (Concord, Mass.). Where the world's deepest meteorite crater may be in Arizona, New England will claim its only marshmallow fluff factory (Lynn, Mass.). Where the tallest tree may be a California redwood, New England counters with the world's smallest church (Wiscasset, Me.). Germany may have the world's oldest brewery (900 years), but New England claims the world's oldest bat (Dorset, Vt.). The New Englander's goal is not exactly to equal the challengers' conventional marvels, but to throw competitors slightly off balance with records that are well enough old or tall or wide or otherwise singular—but that also embody some element of the whimsical or fanciful that outlanders cannot really deal with in their square, head-on approach to world-recordism.

Whether New Englanders' records are really more fun than anybody else's is eventually a matter of personal taste, but there is no doubt that the world at large, as well as many Eastern natives, will be amazed at the riches of the native New England landscape when it comes to record-setting phenomena. Behind the pride looms a question—Why does anybody want to brag about a record in his town, city or village? This is a worldwide trait, though maybe it characterizes the heart-on-sleeve hopefulness and boastfulness of new lands more than it does older societies. Again, some of the bragging on a local record gives a sense of power: My old man can beat up your old man (My bridge is longer than your bridge).

The American sense of straight pride in *bigness* of any kind goes in here as well—bigness as an unquestioned value. Thus, if your town is the residence of the world's heaviest cat (Ridgefield, Conn.), you will probably bring it up at every meeting with a stranger. The fact confers a mysterious uniqueness upon you as well as upon the town and the cat. That uniqueness is what we all want, even soldiers in uniform or nuns in habit. We don't want to be mistaken for somebody else—we want a sense of solidity, of oldtime tradition to bolster our credentials during our short stay on earth. It strengthens our identities if, as New Englanders, we can say with authority that we come from the town where the first earmuffs were manufactured a century ago (Farmington, Me.). If we may indeed sound a bit daft in our vanity to, say, a Midwesterner or some other non-New Englander, we live on in the serene complacency of knowing we have the college that invented and produced the world's largest yo-yo (M.I.T.).

New Englanders have another attraction to records: a simple

love of arcana, the more trivial the better. There is no lack of it; this book offers but a sampling. If this fertile record-breaking soil keeps producing there will be still another record to top all these: New England will be the place where more records of all kinds originate than anywhere else in the world!

Note on Records' Sources. Travel offices and economic development bureaus of the six New England states, chambers of commerce, local newspaper files, schools and colleges, libraries and other local sources lead to many listings of records that also turn up, sometimes in versions differing slightly in some details, in such larger compendia as the *Information Please Almanac, World Almanac, Guinness Book of World Records,* and Joseph Nathan Kane's *Famous First Facts.* The various encyclopedias, and, especially the famous WPA series of state travel guides first published in the early forties and since updated, are studded with little-known records. History books on the states and major cities are also larded with hidden firsts, mosts, greatests and onlies. In fact, idle browsing in almost any printed matter whatever that originates in New England seems to make records leap out of the page. Even immodest billboards, like the one touting the World's Largest Basket Store, outside Putney, Vermont, seem to jump up and down at the arrival of the records hunter. In addition, acquaintances and anybody else hearing about the hunt are immediately eager to add to the records accretion, so that the same record might go into the hopper a dozen times before a final culling has sifted various versions out, ideally, to a single entry per claim. Like that salt box that wouldn't quit and finally filled the sea, once started the flow of records won't be stopped—so be on guard for a future edition of even bigger and narrower and finer and heavier and marvelouser records of every kind.

Foster, Rhode Island   Roy Bongartz
January 1978

Agriculture

America's Most Valuable Cropland. WINDSOR, CONN.: Windsor is the center of the Connecticut River valley tobacco-growing area, where shade-grown tobacco has been produced since 1640. It takes 50 million square yards of cheesecloth, spread on frames over the fields, to shade the tobacco plants. These tobacco fields have the highest value per acre of any U.S. cropland. Most of the tobacco produced from them ends up in cigar wrappers.

NEW ENGLAND'S FARMS AND FARMERS

New England's Most Agricultural State. VERMONT: The Bureau of the Census in 1970 reported that Vermont's farm population was 32,000, more than those of the other New England states. New England as a whole is the least agricultural section of the country, with the lowest farm population (128,000) and the fewest farms (29,000), of the nation's census sections.

1

World's First Concord Grape. CONCORD, MASS.: Ephraim W. Bull developed the famous grape variety here in 1853 and inaugurated commercial production of table grapes in the U.S. Bull lacked the shrewdness to profit from the new grape, and an epitaph on his grave reads: *He sowed, others reaped.*

World's Largest Cranberry Plantation. CARVER, MASS.: The six-mile Edaville Railroad runs through the cranberry bogs here, site of a Cranberry Festival—the world's only such celebration—held in October.

America's Largest Maple Sugar Plant. ST. JOHNSBURY, VT.: Maple Grove, Inc., on Portland Street here occupies a five-acre site and processes more than 2 million pounds of maple sap annually. A Maple Museum is connected with the company.

World's Largest Bean Seed Company. BOMOSEEN, VT.: The Vermont Bean Seed Company here offers for sale a selection of seeds of more than 100 varieties of bean and 30 varieties of pea, "the largest selection available anywhere in the world." Favorite varieties include the Tall Telephone or Alderman Pea, the Rattlesnake Pole Bean and the Garbanzo Bean.

Animals

World's Heaviest Cat. RIDGEFIELD, CONN.: Spice, a ginger and white tom, owned by Mrs. Loren C. Caddell, weighed 43 pounds in 1974. The *Guinness Book of World Records* recognizes Spice as the record-holder for weight. He died from overeating in 1976.

America's Only Affable Asses (unofficial). MAPLETON, ME.: Ailihew's Affable Asses raises donkeys known as spotted asses. Ailihew's is thought to be the only breeder of Affable Asses in the U.S.—perhaps the world.

World's Most Famous Lamb. STERLING, MASS.: It was in Sterling that Mary Sawyer took her sick lamb to school with her one day, an act recorded in the nursery rhyme, "Mary Had a Little Lamb," composed by a local poet. A report says that "when the first phonograph record was made, Thomas Edison, its inventor, was asked to say something into the machine. The first words that came to him were verses of 'Mary Had a Little Lamb,' by John Rowlstone of Sterling."

3

World's Oldest Bat. DORSET, VT.: A little brown bat collected in a cave here in April 1960 had been banded in Massachusetts 24 years earlier.

Nation's First Polar Bear Exhibited. BOSTON, MASS.: On January 18, 1733, a polar bear, the first seen in America, was brought in from Greenland by a Captain Atkins and shown in a large cage at Clark's Wharf in the North End. The nine-months-old cub, named Ursa Major, was shipped to London the next year.

America's First Elephant Exhibited. WORCESTER, MASS.: Columbus, the first elephant seen in America, was put on exhibition here in 1818.

Nation's First Leopard Exhibited. BOSTON, MASS.: On February 2, 1802, Othello Pollard charged 25 cents to see an "import from Bengal" shown outside the Columbian Museum. It was the first leopard seen in the U.S.

Nation's First Lion Exhibited. BOSTON, MASS.: On November 26, 1716, at the house of Captain Arthur Savage on Brattle Street, there was "shewn by William Nichols, a Lyon of Barbary," according to the *Boston Gazette.*

World's First Morgan Horse. RANDOLPH, VT: Named for its owner, Justin Morgan, a singing master of Randolph, the original Morgan horse was foaled in West Springfield, Mass., in

1789, but was brought here in 1795. Justin Morgan died in 1821, but his sons—including the celebrated Sherman, Woodbury and Bulrush—continued the Morgan breed, which is today famous all over the world for versatility and overall quality.

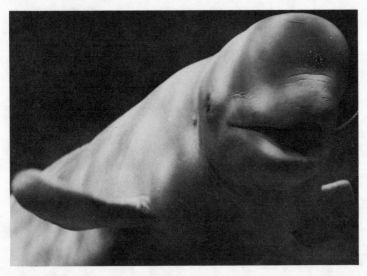

Largest Captive Male Beluga Whale.   *Mystic, Conn.*

World's Largest Male Beluga Whale in Captivity.   MYSTIC, CONN.: Alex, a white whale at Mystic Marinelife, is 13½ feet long and weighs over a ton. He was brought to Mystic from the New York Aquarium in 1976 as a mate for Okie, a female beluga already at Marinelife.

World's Largest Elephant Hide.   MEDFORD, MASS.: The record hide is that of P. T. Barnum's favorite elephant, Jumbo. It is in the Barnum Museum at Tufts University here.

World's Longest Animal. CAPE ANN, MASS.: A giant jelly-fish with a tentacle span of 245 feet and having a 7½-foot bell, was found on the beach here in 1865. The creature is the longest animal on record from anywhere in the world, including extinct species.

World's Largest Lobster. BOSTON, MASS.: The Museum of Science has a stuffed lobster exactly one yard long from tip of claw to tail. It was caught off the Virginia coast in 1934 and weighed 42 pounds, 7 ounces.

America's Most Venerable Sea Monster. LAKE CHAM-PLAIN, VT.: The Lake Champlain Monster, first reported in 1927, has since been sighted repeatedly from the Vermont shore. The *Vermont Life* magazine Monster Editor writes that the monster is reportedly a creature with ". . . three distinct coils, twenty feet in length and with a large globular head (dirty white in color)."

Art & Sculpture

Nation's First Ornamented Soda Fountain. LOWELL, MASS.: Gustavus V. Dows built a white Italian marble soda fountain in 1858, with spread eagles on the syrup taps. In 1862, Dows invented the Double-Stream Draft Arm, allowing a small or large stream of soda to be drawn by the soda jerk.

World's Largest Rocking Horse. WINCHENDON, MASS.: Made in 1914, the wooden horse, 13 feet long and 10½ feet high, is thought to be the biggest in the world. Originally made as the symbol of Winchendon—which is known as "Toy Town" for its many toy factories—the horse now stands on the grounds of the V.F.W. post on Route 12.

America's First Christmas Cards. ROXBURY, MASS.: Louis Prang engraved the first Christmas cards in 1874 for export to England. They were taken in the American trade the following year.

Largest Lipstick (on Tank Treads). *New Haven, Conn.*

World's Largest Reptile Painting. NEW HAVEN, CONN.: A painting entitled "The Age of Reptiles" at Yale University's Peabody Museum here measures 110 feet by 16.

World's Only Statue to Boy Scouts. PLYMOUTH, N.H.: The bronze statue is on the village green here. The statue is a fountain: the scout kneels and the water drips through his hands. It is the work of sculptor George H. Borst, who was a summer resident in the Plymouth area.

First Full-Length Bronze Statue in America. CAMBRIDGE, MASS.: Executed by sculptor Ball Hughes in 1847, the statue was of astronomer Nathaniel Bowditch, seated, holding a copy of his translation of La Place's *Mécanique Celeste* with a globe and quadrant beside him. Placed in Mount Auburn Cemetery, the statue was found imperfect and was re-cast in Paris in 1886.

World's Biggest Lipstick (on Tank Treads). NEW HAVEN, CONN.: Claes Oldenberg's sculpture, *Lipstick,* is on permanent outdoor display at Yale. The lipstick, made of steel, aluminum and fiberglass, stands 22 feet high and weighs about 1¾ tons. It was produced in 1969.

Automobiles

America's First Commercial Auto Maker. SPRINGFIELD, MASS.: Charles Edgar Duryea began making his first car in August 1891, at his shop at 47 Taylor Street here, and first drove it on April 19, 1892. The Duryea Motor Wagon was the first car manufactured regularly for sale in this country, and the Duryea Motor Wagon Co., incorporated in 1895, was the nation's first auto company.

First License Plates. CONNECTICUT: The first permanent automobile license plates were issued by Connecticut beginning on March 1, 1937. The plates were aluminum with black letters.

America's First Steam Auto. BRIDGEPORT, CONN.: A steam-powered car was invented here in 1866 by Henry Alonzo House. House and his partner called their invention a "horseless carriage." It could do 30 miles per hour.

America's First Automobile Accident. NEW YORK, NEW YORK. Although it did not occur in New England, the first auto accident on record involved a New Englander—Henry Wells of SPRINGFIELD, MASS., whose Duryea struck a cyclist on a New York street, May 30, 1896.

Lowest Highway Death Toll. RHODE ISLAND: The computed "mileage death rate" for this state is the nation's lowest: 1.9 deaths per 100 million vehicle miles, according to state traffic authorities (figures for 1975, the latest year for which statistics were available).

America's First Public Garage. BOSTON, MASS.: W. T. McCullough advertised the opening of the Back Bay Cycle and Motor Co. in 1899 as a "stable for renting, sale, storage and repair of motor vehicles."

World's First Automobile Parade. NEWPORT, R.I.: On September 7, 1899, nineteen cars paraded, decorated with flowers and flags, carrying aristocrats of Boston, New York and Philadelphia. A prize was won by Mrs. Hermann Oelrichs, whose auto was overhung with wisteria. Upon the radiator was a flock of pure white doves that appeared to be drawing the vehicle.

World's First Circus To Feature an Automobile as an Attraction. SOUTHERN NEW ENGLAND: In 1864 the Wheeler, Hatch & Hitchcock Circus and Royal Hippodrome, touring Massachusetts, Connecticut and Rhode Island, exhibited a "tremendous novelty, never seen before, of an ordinary road carriage driven over the common highways without the aid of horses or other draught animals, being beyond doubt the most simple, useful and ingenious piece of mechanism ever put into practical use."

America's First Motorist Jailed for Speeding. NEWPORT, R.I.: Justice of the First District Court Darius Baker, on August 28, 1904, sent a speeding second offender to jail after he had already been fined $15 for a first offense—driving 20 miles per hour.

World's First Automobile Race on a Track. CRANSTON, R.I.: On September 7, 1896, at Narragansett Speedway, 40,000 spectators watched five gasoline and two electric cars race. The winner was an electric Riker that posted a speed of 2 minutes, 47 seconds for the mile. The race was for five heats of five miles each, on a one-mile dirt track, one heat to be run on each afternoon of the Rhode Island State Fair.

America's First Speedway. CRANSTON, R.I.: An asphalt-covered automobile raceway—the Narragansett Speedway—was opened here in 1915. Two world's speed records were broken here.

America's First Pneumatic Tire. HARTFORD, CONN.: In 1895 the Hartford Rubber Works made an air-filled auto tire. It was used on the Duryea automobile which won a race sponsored by the Hartford *Times–Herald*.

Nation's Worst Drivers (unofficial). MASSACHUSETTS: *See under* Crime. **Most Car Thefts.**

Aviation

World's First Airplane Flight. BRIDGEPORT, CONN.: Gustave Whitehead, on August 14, 1901, two and a half years before the Wright Brothers' flights at Kittyhawk, made four flights in his airplane, "No. 21." Whitehead's best distance was 1½ miles.

World's First Helicopter. STRATFORD, CONN.: The Vought–Sikorsky Aircraft plant built their model VS–300 in October 1939. On July 18, 1940, Igor Ivan Sikorsky flew a VS–300 for 15 minutes and 3 seconds. The aircraft had a single main rotor powered by a 70-horsepower engine, and three tail rotors for control.

Nation's First Helicopter Air Mail. BRIDGEPORT, CONN.: On July 5, 1946, chief pilot D. D. ("Jimmy") Viner of the Sikorsky Aircraft Company took mail from the post office to the airport in a Sikorsky helicopter.

First Helicopter.   Stratford, Conn.

World's First Nylon Parachute Jump. HARTFORD, CONN.: On June 6, 1942, Miss Adeline Gray, a parachute rigger of the Pioneer Parachute Company, Manchester, Conn., made a jump from an airplane over Brainerd Field here.

World's First Rocket Flight Powered by Liquid Fuel. AUBURN, MASS.: Professor Robert Hutchings Goddard directed a blastoff here on March 16, 1926. An alcohol heater produced internal pressure that sent Goddard's experimental rocket 184 feet into the air in 2½ seconds, a speed of 60 miles per hour. Professor Goddard had been demonstrating the lifting force of combined liquid oxygen and ether in rockets as early as 1920 at nearby Clark University, Worcester, Mass.

Nation's First Aerial Photograph.   BOSTON, MASS.: A photograph taken by J. W. Black from a balloon, *The Queen of the Air,* at a height of 1,200 feet, on October 13, 1860, was entitled "Boston as the Eagle and the Wild Goose See It." The balloon was held in place by a cable. Eight pictures were taken but only one came out. Wet plates were prepared on the spot in the balloon gondola before each exposure.

Baseball

World's First World's Series Baseball Champions. PROVI-
DENCE, R.I.: In 1884 the Providence Grays won the first three
of a best-three-out-of-five series against the Metropolitans of the
American Association. Scores were 6–0, 3–1, 12–2.

**World's First Unassisted Triple Play in Organized Base-
ball.** PROVIDENCE, R.I.: Paul Hines, center fielder, made
the play for the Providence Grays on May 8, 1878, in a game
against Boston. The Grays won, 3–2.

World's Only Baseball Pigeon Rule. BOSTON, MASS.: At
Fenway Park the Pigeon-fly Rule is observed. If a batted ball
strikes one of the thousands of pigeons living in the stadium, the
ball, but not necessarily the pigeon, is ruled dead.

World's First Baseball Glove. BOSTON, MASS.: The glove
was worn by Boston first baseman Charles C. Waite in 1875.

16

There was apparently some question about how use of the glove would be received by fans, for Waite's glove was made in flesh color so as not to attract attention.

THE BOSTON RED SOX

Smallest Major League Stadium. Fenway Park, Home of the Red Sox, is the smallest major league ballpark in the U.S., with a seating capacity of 33,437 (the Montreal Expos stadium is smaller, however). The Fenway also has the shortest right field fence in the majors—302 feet.

Most R.B.I. Leaders. The Red Sox have had the American League Runs Batted In leader seven times—more than any other team in either league. Ted Williams of the Red Sox was American League R.B.I. leader four times, more than any other player in either league. In 1949 Williams and Vern Stephens, also of Boston, each batted in 159 runs—a major league record that stands today.

Most Two-Base Hits in a Season. In 1931 Earl Webb of the Red Sox hit 67 doubles, the major league record.

World's First Baseball Catcher's Mask. LYNN, MASS.: Patented by Winthrop Thayer of Waverly, Mass., the mask was first used in a game here on April 12, 1877 between the Live Oaks and the Harvard Baseball Club.

World's First Intercollegiate Baseball Game. PITTSFIELD, MASS.: On July 1, 1859, Amherst College beat Williams College 66–32 in a 26-inning game. There were 13 players on each team.

World's Only National Women's Softball Tournament. STRATFORD, CONN.: The playoff is held at Raybestos Memorial Field here each August. Among contesting teams are the Bloomer Girls, of Cleveland; the Jax Maids, of New Orleans; the Lionettes, of Orange, Calif.; the Betsy Ross Rockets, of Fresno, Calif.; the Arizona Ramblers, of Phoenix; and the Raybestos Brakettes, of Stratford. Since the first championship playoff in 1933, the Brakettes have been champions in 14 seasons, including every year from 1971 through 1977.

Basketball

World's First College Basketball Game. NEW HAVEN, CONN.: Wesleyan University's seven-man team beat Yale's 4–3 here on December 10, 1896.

THE BOSTON CELTICS

Most NBA Championships. The Celtics have won the National Basketball Association championship playoffs 11 times, more than any other team. They have also won more consecutive NBA playoffs than any other team—eight, between 1959 and 1966.

Most Conference Championships. The Celtics have won their conference or division championship 14 times, more than any other team. They won the eastern conference nine years in a row (1957 to 1965)—another record.

Most Thousand-Point Seasons. Total team points scored by the Celtics have exceeded 1,000 in 14 seasons, a scoring record.

World's First Basketball Game. SPRINGFIELD, MASS.:
The game was introduced here by James Naismith in 1892 at a
YMCA training school. The **World's Only Basketball Hall of
Fame** is in Springfield.

Birds

America's First Bird Sanctuary. MERIDEN, N.H.: The Helen Woodruff Smith Sanctuary here was established in 1910. It comprises 32 acres of forest and meadow. The Sanctuary was founded by Ernest Harold Baynes, a Meriden naturalist.

First Proven Transatlantic Bird Flight. EASTERN EGG ROCK, ME.: A common tern, banded here on July 3, 1913, was found dead in August 1917 at the mouth of the Niger River in West Africa. This was the first record of a bird having crossed the Atlantic.

America's First Chicken Show. BOSTON, MASS.: The Grand Show of Domestic Poultry and Convention of Fowl Breeders and Fanciers was held in 1849 at the Public Garden. On exhibition were 1,423 chickens in 219 cages.

America's Most Celebrated Bird-Watcher. OLD LYME, CONN.: Roger Tory Peterson, 69, of Old Lyme is one of the

world's leading ornithologists and bird artists. Peterson's *Field
Guide to the Birds,* first published in 1934, has had 47 printings.
With over a million copies in print, *A Field Guide to the Birds* is
one of the few really indispensable books in any field. Peterson is
also the author or co-author of some 15 other books, as well as
scores of articles, on American and European birds. He has received awards, prizes and honorary degrees from many institutions in the U.S. and Europe.

Only Lead Balloon That Goes Over.   *Cambridge, Mass.* ▶

Blimps

First Goodyear Blimp. EAST WALPOLE, MASS.: On May 22, 1930, a Goodyear dirigible was chartered by Bird & Son, Inc. as a "good-will messenger." The blimp made 1,380 flights in five months, carrying 6,000 passengers altogether.

First Dirigible Brokerage. PORTLAND, ME.: The first stock order ever called in from a dirigible was relayed to Portland on August 8, 1930 by Alexander Godfrey of Boston, who was aloft in the *Graf Zeppelin* when he felt the impulse to trade.

World's Only Lead Balloon That Does Go Over. CAMBRIDGE, MASS.: A 450-cubic-foot helium-filled balloon with a skin of lead foil $7/16$ millimeter thick was successfully launched on May 16, 1976 from the headquarters of the Arthur D. Little, Inc., research center here. In another attempt, scientists here also tried to send up a square balloon, but the 729-cubic-foot craft ripped apart in the wind before rising from the ground.

Books

World's Fastest Book Printing Job. CLINTON, MASS.: In 1963 the Colonial Press here printed 500,000 copies of the Warren Commission Report on the Kennedy assassination in 45 hours.

Nation's First Cookbook. HARTFORD, CONN.: Amelia Simmons had a 46-page cookbook printed here in 1796. Its title: *American Cookery, or the Art of Dressing Viands, Fish, Poultry and Vegetables, and the Best Modes of Making Puff-Pastes, Pies, Tarts, Puddings, Custards and Preserves, and all Kinds of Cakes, From the Imperial Plumb to Plain Cake—Adapted to This Country, and All Grades of Life—*an unofficial world's record for **Longest Cookbook Title.**

America's First Fishing Book. BOSTON, MASS.: A how-to book for fishermen was published in 1743 for Samuel Kneeland and Timothy Green. Its title, *A discourse utter'd in Part at Ammaukeeg-Falls, in the fishing-season 1739.*

Nation's Only Town History To Be Awarded the Pulitzer Prize. SUDBURY, MASS.: Sumner Chilton Powell won a Pulitzer in 1964 for his book, *Sudbury, Puritan Village: The Formation of a New England Town.*

America's First Novel. WORCESTER, MASS.: *The Power of Sympathy,* by William Hill Brown, was published here in 1789. The two-volume work was dedicated "to the young ladies of America."

Bridges

America's First Bridge. MILTON, MASS.: Israel Stoughton bridged the Neponset River from here to Dorchester in 1634.

America's First Toll Bridge. ROWLEY, MASS.: Richard Thurlow built a toll bridge at his own expense across the Newbury River, and on May 3, 1654, the General Court of Massachusetts fixed tolls for animals. People could pass free.

America's First Pile Bridge. YORK, ME.: Designed and built by Major Samuel Sewall in 1761, the bridge consisted of 13 groups of piles set into the bed of the York River. A 270-foot wooden bridge was placed atop the piles.

World's Widest Bridge. PROVIDENCE, R.I.: The Crawford Street Bridge is 1,147 feet wide. Earlier called the Weybosset Bridge, first built in 1711, the present structure was completed in 1930 and was built in six separate units: the Crawford bridge,

557 feet; the Weybosset bridge, 170 feet; the Washington Row bridge, 170 feet; and the Burnside, Post Office and Exchange bridges totaling 250 feet.

NEW ENGLAND'S BRIDGES

New England's Longest Bridge.   NEWPORT, R.I.: The Newport Bridge over Narragansett Bay here is 1,600 feet long. It was finished in 1969.

Second Longest Bridge is also in Rhode Island: the Mount Hope Bridge (1,200 feet), completed in 1929.

Nation's First Pontoon Bridge.   LYNN, MASS.: Captain Moses Brown was instructed to bridge Collins Pond in 1804. The pond was deep and had a soft bottom which precluded the use of piers. Brown's bridge, when floated into place, was 511 feet long and 28 feet wide.

Nation's Oldest Covered Bridge.   MIDDLEBURY, VT.: The Pulp Mill Bridge over Otter Creek here was built about 1820. The bridge, of Burr truss construction, covers 179 feet in three spans.

Ruggedest Covered Bridges.   PITTSFORD, VT.: The Hammond Bridge and the Gorham Bridge here washed out and floated down Otter Creek in the Great Flood of 1927. After the deluge, both bridges were found, returned, and put in use again.

America's Only Honeycomb Granite Bridge. ORR'S IS-LAND, ME.: The Bailey Island Bridge is built of unmortared granite blocks laid up so as to leave spaces between blocks. This allows tides to pass through the bridge's structure rather than beat against it. There is only one other bridge of this type in the world, located in Scotland.

America's Longest Covered Bridge. CORNISH, N.H.: Built in 1866, the great bridge over the Connecticut River between Cornish and Windsor, Vermont, is 460 feet long. It was a toll bridge until 1943 (two cents for a pedestrian; a half cent if the pedestrian was a sheep). Though only seven feet of the bridge lie in Windsor (because of the location of the New Hampshire border), Vermonters often claim the bridge for their own: "It ends in Vermont," they say.

Longest Covered Bridge.   Cornish, N.H.

Buildings

Nation's Oldest Public Building. YORK, ME.: The Old Gaol, now a museum, was built in 1653.

America's First Lighthouse. BOSTON, MASS.: The Boston Light was erected in 1716 on what is now Little Brewster Island in Boston Harbor. The first light keeper was lost at sea with his wife and daughter, an event which Benjamin Franklin, then twelve, made the subject of a poem, "Lighthouse Tragedy." Boston Light was blown up by the British in 1776.

Nation's First Windowless Factory. FITCHBURG, MASS.: The Simonds Saw and Steel Company built a one-story factory in 1930 that had no skylights but was lighted by hundreds of 1,000-watt bulbs. Black floors contrasted with walls painted orange, blue and green. Ten million cubic feet of air, purified, heated and humidified, was circulated through the plant every ten minutes. Cork pads deadened sound in the building. Cost of construction was $1.5 million.

Oldest Public Building.   York, Me.

Nation's Longest Greenhouse. GUILFORD, CONN.: Pinchbeck's Rose Farm has a glass house 81 feet wide and 1,200 feet long, the largest single-span iron-framed greenhouse in the U.S. Temperatures of 80 degrees daytime and 60 at night are provided in cold weather by boilers consuming 300,000 gallons of oil a year. Founded by William Pinchbeck, Jr., in 1929, the business is now operated by the founder's grandson, William W. Pinchbeck. The greenhouses have 95,000 rose bushes that produce three million blooms every year; the bushes are cut twice daily year around. Over eighty per cent of all the Pinchbeck roses are red.

Nation's Only Combination Jail and Hotel. NEWFANE, VT.: In the 2½-story Windham County Jail, trusties used to have meals with the guests in the dining room. Opened as a jail, by 1900 the building also housed paying guests who had traveled to Newfane for court business and had nowhere to stay. The operation closed in 1945, and the jail is used as a residence today, the hotel part having been torn down in 1956.

World's Largest Colonial-Style Office Building. HARTFORD, CONN.: The home of the Aetna Life Affiliated Company (insurance) here is 660 feet long. The main building is six stories high. The building was designed by James Gambel Rogers and built in 1929.

World's Largest Shore Dinner Hall. ROCKY POINT, R.I.: The famous shore dinner hall at Rocky Point Amusement Park, which opened in 1847, can serve 600 gallons of clam chowder in a single hour to a capacity seafood-eating crowd of 4,000. On a good day five tons of clamcakes, shot out of a special clamcake cannon invented here, will disappear down the gullets of gourmands. In a vast building 100 yards long that has been rebuilt twice after hurricanes destroyed it earlier this century, chowderhounds sit along 20-foot tables to devour the official shore dinner, the menu for which is unchanged since 1847, and includes Bermuda onions, relishes, olives, cucumbers, chowder (with tomatoes in the Rhode Island style), white and brown bread, baked clams, drawn butter, clamcakes, baked fish, french fries, creole sauce, baked sausage, corn on the cob, boiled lobster, watermelon, and Indian pudding. The record number of diners, served during a hot summer day in 1975, was 37,075.

Nation's First Building Devoted Entirely To Highway Traffic. SAUGATUCK, CONN.: The Eno Foundation for Highway Traffic Control, Inc., completed its building here on July 1, 1939.

NEW ENGLAND'S TALL BUILDINGS

New England's Tallest Building. BOSTON, MASS.: The John Hancock Tower (790 feet high, 60 stories) was designed by architect I. M. Pei and completed in 1972. It is the tallest building north of New York.

New England's Second Tallest Building. Also in Boston, the Prudential Building, built in 1965, is 750 feet high in 52 stories. On a clear day you can see Mt. Monadnock in New Hampshire from the observation area atop The Prudential—a look of 60 miles.

World's First Quonset Hut. DAVISVILLE, R.I.: Built in 1941 at the Quonset Point air station for the U.S. Navy by the Great Lakes Steel Corp., the huts were constructed around a framework of steel material that had a groove into which nails could be driven. The Navy calls them Arch-Rib Huts, officially.

America's Most Elaborate Log Cabin. JACKMAN, ME.: The main building at the Sky Lodge, in Moose River near here, is a four-story structure built of spruce logs. Begun in 1929, the lodge has eleven bedrooms, dining room, library and pantry; plus ten fireplaces, one of them in the bathroom of the master suite. The main room is 50 by 40 feet with twin bow staircases

Most Elaborate Log Cabin.   Jackman, Me.

(called "the welcoming arms") and a cathedral ceiling. The cost of construction was $135,000—which, as a local historian has noted, was a lot of money in 1929.

America's Only Tavern Featuring Asparagus Fly-Catchers (unofficial). NORTH SMITHFIELD, R.I.: The Seth Allen Tavern on Great Road, built in 1804, was equipped with wire hooks on which bunches of asparagus were hung to catch flies.

World's Largest Gym. NEW HAVEN, CONN.: The Cathedral of Muscle, Yale University's Payne Whitney Gymnasium, is nine stories tall, with wings of five stories, and has four basket-

Largest Gym.   New Haven, Conn.

ball courts, twelve handball courts, a roof running track, a 25-yard swimming pool on one floor and a 55-yard pool on another, three rowing tanks, and 28 squash courts. The building was completed in 1932.

Chairs

World's Largest Chair. GARDNER, MASS.: On July 4, 1976, the Gardner Rotary Club presented as a gift to the city a ladderback chair 20 feet, 7 inches tall, 14 inches wide, and 9 feet deep. The chair is made of turned Honduras mahogany. It weighs 3,000 pounds. Mr. N. D. Rudziak of Gardner Rotary says: "A survey was conducted of all large chairs throughout the nation known to be in existence to insure that when completed it would in fact be the world's largest." Gardner is Chair City of the World.

World's Second Largest Chair. BENNINGTON, VT.: A chair at the Haynes & Kane furniture store here is 19 feet, 1 inch tall and weighs 2,200 pounds.

Churches

America's Only Sixteen-Sided Church. RICHMOND, VT.: The Old Round Church, built in 1813, was the first community church in the U.S. to be used by different sects. Founders included Congregationalists, Universalists, Baptists and Methodists. The groups squabbled and departed from the church one by one until the building became the Richmond town hall. It was an octagonal belfry. An offer from Henry Ford to buy the structure and remove it to Dearborn Village museum in Michigan was turned down by the townspeople.

Nation's First Gothic Building. NEW HAVEN, CONN.: Trinity Episcopal Church, designed by Ithiel Town in 1814, was built of traprock (basalt) with brownstone trim.

World's Smallest Church. WISCASSET, ME.: The Union Church measures 7 by 4½ feet. The church was built in 1957 by the Rev. Louis W. West, who regularly conducted morning prayer, weddings and child dedications in the little church. Rev.

West died in 1966; the Union Church is maintained in his memory.

Nation's Only Church on a State Line. BLACKSTONE, MASS.: At St. Paul's Church here, built in 1852, the organ is played in Massachusetts and the sound comes out in Rhode Island.

America's Oldest Baptist Church. PROVIDENCE, R.I.: The First Baptist Meeting House, built in 1775, had a novel steeple and bell that earlier churches of this denomination avoided in their buildings.

World's First Movable Church. JAMESTOWN ISLAND, R.I.: The Chapel of the Transfiguration, consecrated on June 3, 1899, measured 27 by 18 feet and had 14 benches, 20 chairs, a platform, and an altar. The interior, including the pews, prayer desk and altar, was made of oak. The chapel was built on a wooden chassis with four wheels and was drawn from place to place by horses. The first preacher was the Rev. Charles E. Preston of St. Matthews Church, who held the first service in the chapel on April 23, 1899.

World's Only Children's Church. MILTON, MASS.: The Children's Church (Unitarian), 18 by 32 feet, with a steeple, belfry, organ, spire and pews, was dedicated on November 14, 1937, by the Rev. Vivian Towse Pomeroy. Costing over $5,000, the church had its own pastor, the Rev. Mrs. Dorothy Pomeroy.

World's First Steeple on a Methodist Church.   NEWPORT,
R.I.: St. Paul's Methodist Church on Marlborough Street was
the first of its denomination to get a steeple, in 1806.

World's Only Steeple Clock To Ring Ship's Time.   WELL-
FLEET, MASS.: The First Congregational Church here, built
in 1850, rings only ship's time. The steeple tolls the watches—
one to eight bells, struck on the half hour, 48 times around the
clock. Sunday chime concerts are given in summer.

Cities & Towns

Nation's First City. NEW HAVEN, CONN.; HARTFORD,
CONN.: Developing from settlements first named in 1640 and
1636, respectively, New Haven and Hartford were both incorporated as cities in 1784, adding fuel to the rivalry between
them.

**America's Only Town Named as the Result of a Fist
Fight.** BARRE, VT.: In 1793, according to a well-known local
story, at a meeting called to name the town, two men from
Massachusetts, one Thompson of Holden and one Sherman
from Barre, fought over naming the Vermont place for their
home towns. Thompson was knocked out, upon which Sherman
cried, "There, by God, the name is Barre!"

**Nation's Only Town To Give Commissions to Pi-
rates.** NEWPORT, R.I.: During Newport's private war with
the Dutch in 1653—not entered by any of the rest of the Ameri-

can colonies—commissions were paid to pirates for the capture
of Dutch ships.

Nation's Smallest City.   VERGENNES, VT.: The city's area
is one square mile, its population 2,242 (1970). Vergennes is the
third oldest incorporated city in the U.S., having been chartered
in 1788.

America's Best Represented Town (unofficial). ST.
GEORGE, VT.: One of every four residents of St. George (population 110) holds political office.

America's Most Illustrious Townsmen.   BELMONT, MASS.:
Belmont (population 28,000), claims to have more residents, per
capita, listed in *Who's Who In America* than any other town in the
U.S.

**America's Most Jurisdictionally Confusing City (unoffi-
cial).**   RUTLAND, VT.: Rutland City is surrounded by Rutland Town. Rutland City has a mayor, while the larger but
more sparsely populated Town of Rutland has its own separate
town government. Center Rutland is the chief settlement within
Rutland Town (it is not to be confused with Rutland City).
West Rutland is a separate town with its own government, distinct from those of Center Rutland, Rutland Town and Rutland City.

America's Largest Manchester.   MANCHESTER, N.H.: This
is one of the commonest place names in the U.S.; there are 33
Manchesters. Manchester, N.H. (population 87,754) is the
largest.

America's Only City To Play Host at the Formal End of a Foreign War. PORTSMOUTH, N.H.: In 1905 Portsmouth was the scene of the signing of the treaty ending the Russo–Japanese War. President Theodore Roosevelt presided at the peace ceremonies.

Nation's First Local Speeding Law. NEWPORT, R.I.: In 1678 the Rhode Island General Assembly, in session here, passed a law banning the galloping of horses through town streets.

Clothing & Materials

World's First Felt. NEWPORT, R.I.: Thomas Robinson Williams invented the process of felt manufacture in 1820. Wool was carded and placed in layers with the finest on the outside. The wool was then immersed in water and agitated, while rollers squeezed it and hammers beat it.

America's First Derby Hat. SOUTH NORWALK, CONN.: Made by James Henry Knapp in 1850, the hats were named for the English horse race. The first order for derbies, half a dozen each of brown and black, went to a store at Broadway and Ninth Street, New York City.

Button Capital of the World. WATERBURY, CONN.: As early as 1790 the Grilley brothers had opened a factory here for the casting of pewter buttons, the first such factory in the U.S. Abel Porter & Co. made gilt-faced buttons here in 1802, another first.

Nation's First Cloth-Covered Buttons. EASTHAMPTON, MASS.: Mrs. Samuel Williston made covered buttons here in 1826, after which her husband and his associate, Joel Hayden, invented a cloth-covered-button-making machine and introduced the product commercially. The partnership between Williston and Hayden endured until 1848, at which time Williston bought out his partner.

World's First Fitted Horseblankets. TROY, N.H.: Beginning in 1852 Thomas Goodall made blankets cut to fit the horse and attached buckles for securing them.

World's First Arctics. DORCHESTER, MASS.: Thomas Crane Wales obtained a patent on waterproof boots and gaiters on February 2, 1858. His product was known as Wales Patent Arctic Gaiter, and was made of rubber and cloth.

Nation's First Shoe Measuring Stick. STAMFORD, CONN.: In 1657, during a court dispute in New Haven over shoe sizes, the judge was told that William Newman of Stamford had an instrument "which is thought to be right to determine the question between the buyer and seller," and the court ordered the stick brought in.

World's Only Hog Shoes. PERU, MASS.: A historical guide says: "In 1799 Charles Ford moved to Peru with a horse, cart, yoke of oxen and one dog, as well as a hog. Since the hog had to walk it became footsore and caused much delay. Shoemaker Ford sat down by the roadside and made boots of sole leather for the hog."

World's First Earmuffs. FARMINGTON, ME.: Chester Greenwood invented earmuffs here in 1873. Greenwood's prototype was ear-shaped fur pieces wired to a bowler hat. He later went into production with Greenwood's Champion Ear Protectors (patent 1877).

Collections

World's Largest Collection of Elephant Hair. HARTFORD, CONN.: Charles Davis of Hartford has a collection that includes hair from 500 elephants. An elephant has only between five and eight hairs on its body.

Nation's Biggest Collection of Old Newspapers. WORCESTER, MASS.: The newspaper file of the American Antiquarian Society here has over three million copies, mainly from the period 1690–1820. Included are the complete files of the Boston *Evening Post* (1735–1775), the *American Weekly Mercury* (1719–1746), the New York *Weekly Journal* (1773–1751) and the *Pennsylvania Gazette* (1735–1775). U.S. newspapers from the East Coast and Mississippi Valley are filed up to 1876, from the Plains States to 1880, from the Rocky Mountain States to 1890, and from the Southwest to 1895. Alaska papers go up to 1900. Among treasures is the George P. Rowell Collection, assembled for the Newspaper Pavilion of the Centennial Exposition at Philadelphia in 1876, including a copy of every newspaper and periodical published in the U.S. in that year.

Biggest Armor Collection.   Worcester, Mass.

Nation's Biggest Private Collection of Armor. WORCES-
TER, MASS.: The John Higgins Armory at the Worcester
Pressed Steel Company here occupies a four-story building that
contains 400 complete suits of medieval armor. The 3,000 exhibits run from stone age weapons through Roman gladiators'
trappings and chain mail.

World's Largest Tree Collection. BOSTON, MASS.: Harvard University's Arnold Arboretum here has the world's largest
collection of trees and shrubs—all labeled with name and date—
in grounds covering several hundred acres. The Arboretum,
which was endowed in 1872, is open to the public as a park.

Commerce

America's First Export of Ice. BOSTON, MASS.: In August 1805 Frederick Tudor sent 130 tons of ice to Martinique aboard the brig *Favorite*. By 1833 Tudor was shipping ice to India, to the ice markets of Calcutta, Bombay and Madras.

World's Largest Basket Store. PUTNEY, VT.: The Basketville store here, opened in 1956, sells about 100,000 baskets annually from a store occupying 15,000 square feet. Eighty employees manufacture most of Basketville's baskets, buckets and other woodenware, much of it in a factory across the road from the store.

World's Largest Lecture Agency. CHESTNUT HILL, MASS.: The American Program Bureau represents 500 lecturers and handles over $5 million a year. Lecturers available through the Bureau are a diverse lot, which includes: E. Howard Hunt, Joe Namath, Art Linkletter, Ralph Nader, the Fonz, Ronald Reagan, Jimmy the Greek, Sen. J. Strom Thurmond, and the Danish Gym Team.

Crime

America's First Bank Robbery. CONCORD, MASS.: Robber Langdon W. Moore, on September 25, 1865, got away with $310,000 from the National Bank here.

America's Biggest Robbery. PLYMOUTH, MASS.: On August 14, 1962, a U.S. Mail truck was robbed of $1,551,277, cash, near Plymouth. This is the biggest haul in the annals of American crime.

America's First Duel. PLYMOUTH, MASS.: The first duel fought on American soil was enacted, not by high-spirited Virginians, as might be expected, but by mild Pilgrims of Plymouth Colony. Edward Leister and Edward Dotey, servingmen, fought with swords and daggers on June 18, 1621. Dotey was wounded on the hand, and Leister on the thigh. The government of the colony took a dim view. The duelists were sentenced to be bound together, head to head and feet to feet, and held so for 24 hours.

America's First Execution. PLYMOUTH, MASS.: John Billington, a signer of the Pilgrims' compact, was hanged here for murder on September 30, 1630. Billington had shot and killed John Newcomin in a quarrel.

Nation's First Deportation. MARE MOUNT, MASS.: Thomas Morton was deported from his residence here to England on June 9, 1628, in the custody of John Oldham. He was charged with living "with a licentious group" and of trading guns to Indians.

America's First Disbarment. BOSTON, MASS.: Lawyer Thomas Lechford was disbarred by the General Court of Massachusetts in 1639. Lechford was convicted of attempting to influence members of the jury out of court. He was pardoned for this offense, but was disbarred again a year later, again for jury tampering. He was then pardoned for the second offense, too. Then as now, it was hard to keep a lawyer out of work.

America's Busiest Firebugs. BOSTON, MASS.: Thirty-three were indicted here in October 1977 for allegedly participating in what a United Press report called the largest arson ring ever uncovered in the United States. Among those charged were real estate operators, lawyers, wealthy landlords, restaurateurs, a plumber, and a former captain in the Boston Fire Department arson squad, according to UPI.

America's First Prostitute. QUINCY, MASS.: Styled "this goodly creature of incontinency," the unnamed female figure in

Thomas Morton's "licentious" colony in Quincy, was noted in Morton's *New English Canaan,* a book he published in 1637.

America's First Pirate. BRISTOL, ME.: Dixie Bull looted Bristol in 1632. Earlier, he had received a land grant at York, Me. Bull turned to piracy when the French seized a shallop of his in Penobscot Bay and made off with its contents.

Most Car Thefts. MASSACHUSETTS: The rate of auto thefts in Massachusetts is the highest in the U.S.: 1,571 thefts per 100,000 population in 1975 (the latest year for which figures are available). Rhode Island is number two. This may explain the notoriety Massachusetts residents have gained as the **Nation's Worst Drivers (unofficial).** If Bay State motorists are reckless on the road, perhaps it's because they are often driving someone else's car.

Electrical Devices

World's First Electric Motor. BRANDON, VT.: Thomas Davenport built a crude electric motor in his blacksmith shop here in 1834. Four magnets and a battery were assembled to spin a wheel in Davenport's invention. Another Vermonter, Wareham Chase of Calais, built a similar device around the same time. Chase and Davenport did not know of each other's work.

America's First Burglar Alarm. BOSTON, MASS.: The nation's first burglar alarm was installed here by Edwin Thomas Holmes on February 21, 1858. It operated when the release of a spring, caused by the opening of a door or window, made an electrical contact.

World's First Pull-Chain Electric Light. BRIDGEPORT, CONN.: Harvey Hubbell patented a socket with a pull-chain switch of his invention in 1896.

World's First Electric Light in a Private House. SALEM, MASS.: Professor Moses G. Farmer set up a system of light bulbs in the parlor of his house here in July 1859. The system took power from batteries in the cellar. Prof. Farmer's is thought to have been the first house to use electric light.

World's First Electric Shaver. STAMFORD, CONN.: Colonel Jacob Shick patented an electric "shaving implement" in 1928. The first shavers were manufactured in March 1931.

Events & Gatherings

Biggest Fair East of the Mississippi. SPRINGFIELD, MASS.: The Eastern States' Agricultural and Industrial Exposition occupies grounds of 175 acres. The annual event is held in September and attracts over 1,000 exhibitors.

America's First Fair. DUXBURY, MASS.: An annual fair, the first event of its kind in America, was held in Duxbury beginning in 1638.

Nation's Only Annual World's Fair. TUNBRIDGE, VT.: The Tunbridge World's Fair has been held each September for 100 years. Square dancing, agricultural exhibits and antique sales are featured. "The carnival spirit runs rampant," according to a guidebook: at 3 P.M., it is reported, all sober persons are asked to leave the fair grounds.

Nation's Largest Amateur Telescope-Makers' Convention. SPRINGFIELD, VT.: Astronomer Russell W. Porter organized the Springfield Telescope Makers in 1923. Several hundred telescopists from all over the U.S. and Canada meet at Stellafane Observatory here every summer.

America's Only Dowsers' Convention. DANVILLE, VT.: The American Society of Dowsers has its annual convention here in October. The society was founded in 1961, but meetings of dowsers have been held in Danville for 90 years.

Factories

America's First Cigar Factory. WEST SUFFIELD, CONN.:
Simon Viets built a factory here in 1810 and employed 15
women and a foreman to manufacture cigars under the brand
names "Windsors" and "Long Nines."

Nation's First Nut and Bolt Factory. MARION, CONN.:
Micah Rugg, a blacksmith, and his associate Martin Barnes,
opened a factory in 1840—a single story wooden building measuring 30 by 20 feet. Rugg and Barnes' factory could make 500
bolts a day. Before this, bolts were hammered out by hand.

Nation's First Hat Factory. DANBURY, CONN.: Zadoc
Benedict established the plant in 1780, employing three workers
to make 18 hats a week, of rabbit or beaver fur. Hats sold at
from $6 to $10. They were described as "without elegance,
heavy, rough and unwieldy."

Nation's First Chair Factory. RIVERTON, CONN.: Lambert Hitchcock established a factory here in 1818. The building, restored in 1946, still stands and is used as a factory and retail store.

America's First Baby Carriage Factory. LEOMINSTER, MASS.: Opened in 1858, the F. W. & F. A. Whitney Carriage Company manufactured the first baby carriages in the U.S. Whitney's carriages had "two wheels, with a long tongue and supporting standard in front, made of wood." The first year 75 carriages were built.

America's First Bicycle Factory. HARTFORD, CONN.: The Pope Manufacturing Company began producing "Columbia" bicycles here in 1877. A local sewing machine company carried out the actual manufacture of the bicycles.

World's Only Dandelion Greens Cannery. WILTON, ME.: W. S. Wells & Son here puts up Belle of Maine label greens for wholesale shipments in cases of twelve 15-ounce cans. The firm was founded in 1906.

Nation's First Candle Factory. NEWPORT, R.I.: Benjamin Crabb established a spermaceti candle factory here in 1748. It burned down two years later.

America's First Screw Factory. CRANSTON, R.I.: The firm of Aborn & Jackson began making screws here in 1810. Before the advent of this factory, screws were made laboriously one at a time: blanks were forged and threads were filed by hand.

World's Largest Artificial Flower Company. PROVIDENCE, R.I.: The California Artificial Flower Co. makes some 800,000 flowers a year. Founded in 1921 to make fibre roses and paper flowers, by 1939 the company had 1,000 employees. During World War II the firm had to make military equipment for the government, with but 50 employees permitted to continue making artificial flowers.

America's First Sardine Cannery. EASTPORT, ME.: Julius Wolff established the cannery in 1876. Sardines were packed and sealed in metal cans similar to ones in use today.

World's Only Operating Water-Powered Commercial Snuff Mill. BYFIELD, MASS. The Byfield Snuff Company, operated by a water wheel in the Parker River, has been in operation since 1804. Founded by Benjamin Pearson, the firm has been in the Pearson family continuously since. The present president is in the tenth generation of Pearsons who have run the mill. He is Benjamin Pearson IX. Conveyors, elevators, and cutting machines are directly belted from the water-driven drive shafts.

World's Only Marshmallow Fluff Factory. LYNN, MASS.: Durkee–Mower, Inc., makes 15 million pounds of white glop annually, distributed throughout the eastern half of the U.S. Marshmallow Fluff, the firm's only product, was invented here in 1920 by founders H. Alan Durkee and Fred L. Mower, who originally styled it Toot Sweet Marshmallow Fluff. A. Bruce

Only Up-and-Down Sawmill.   Ledyard, Conn.

Durkee, president of the firm and son of the founder, employs 25 people to make all this Fluff. Of the annual output, Durkee comments, "We've never figured it out, but it might be enough to fill some place like Yankee Stadium." Only one variant of Fluff, a raspberry-flavored kind, is made, and this is shipped only to Vermont. "We really don't know why they like the raspberry Fluff," says Durkee. "The only thing we can figure is that they want people to think they're eating homemade jelly while they're actually eating Marshmallow Fluff."

America's Only Water-Powered Up-and-Down Sawmill. LEDYARD, CONN.: In Colonial America up-and-down saws were the usual type; today this is thought to be the only one remaining in operation. The town of Ledyard owns it and keeps it and the sawmill on Iron Street open for use by the public. Bring your own wood.

Feats

World's Longest Human Ice Encasement. BOSTON, MASS.: Jim Randi stripped naked and entombed himself in ice for 43 minutes and 8 seconds on August 31, 1974.

World's Fastest Mile on Snowshoes. NEW HAVEN, CONN.: On February 19, 1939, Clifford Cody snowshoed a mile in 5 minutes, 18.6 seconds.

World's Longest Crocheted Chain. MERIDEN, CONN.: Lisa Zwolinsky and Chris Kuchalla made a four-ply wool crocheted chain 2.46 miles long in five months, completing it on May 3, 1975. This is the longest such chain on record, according to the *Guinness Book of World Records*. It is now in the Zwolinsky's cellar.

World's Only Attempt To Pull an Island Out of a River. AUGUSTA, ME.: In 1820 an effort was made to drag

Cushnoc Island out of the Kennebec River to facilitate navigation. A report says "one hundred yoke of oxen were procured, mill chains were fastened around the island and linked with the team, and the oxen headed upstream along the riverbank. The first terrific pull succeeded only in throwing the hindmost yoke of oxen into the river. Subsequent efforts throughout the day effected no more than broken chains and crescendoes of curses." The island is still in place.

Firearms

World's First Metal Cartridge. SPRINGFIELD, MASS.: Daniel B. Wesson of the Smith & Wesson Company here invented a successful, self-contained metal cartridge in 1854.

World's First Machine Gun. LOWELL, MASS.: Charles E. Barnes of Lowell patented a crank-operated "automatic cannon" in 1856 which anticipated the famous Gatling Gun by six years.

World's Largest Collection of Small Arms. SPRINGFIELD, MASS.: The Springfield Armory, established in 1794 and retired from service in 1968, has 25,000 specimens of military small arms from all over the world. The first Springfield musket, a flintlock bored for a .69 caliber ball projectile, was made here in 1795. The Armory was sole supplier of U.S. Government small arms between the time of the Civil War and 1904. The most famous display here is the "Organ of Guns," made famous by the Longfellow poem, "The Arsenal at Springfield." Racks of Springfield rifles are arranged like organ pipes. The collection has one of every type of gun manufactured at the armory, from the early musket to the M-14 automatic rifle currently in use by U.S. forces. A display traces the evolution of firearms from the world's first hand gun, a hand cannon made around 1400 A.D. Open daily, the Armory museum is run by the National Park Service.

World's First Bazooka. BRIDGEPORT, CONN.: The Bazooka, a rocket launcher for use against tanks and other armored vehicles, was first produced by the General Electric Company here in 1942. The prototype was a 4-foot steel tube, 2½ inches in diameter, which fired a 2-foot rocket. The weapon was named after a crude gas-pipe horn used by the American comic, Bob Burns.

Fish & Fishing

Sardine Capital.   MAINE: The state leads the U.S. in sardines harvested and packed—150 million cans in 1977.

America's First Government Fish Hatchery.   BUCKSPORT, ME.: A hatchery was opened here in 1872 for propagation of Atlantic salmon. Three New England states co-operated to administer the hatchery, which is still in operation.

World's Only Salmon Pool Within City Limits.   BANGOR, ME.: The Bangor Salmon Pool on the Penobscot River a mile north of the center of town is famous for its tradition of sending the first salmon of each season to the President.

World's First Spoon Fishing Lure.   BOMOSEEN, VT.: The spoon fishing lure was invented here in 1830 by a farm boy, Julio T. Buel. While fishing in Lake Bomoseen, Julio dropped one of his mother's silver spoons overboard, saw a big fish grab it, and ran home to get another.

Record-Setting Game Fish in New England

Blue Shark. ROCKPORT, MASS.: The world's record blue shark, weighing 410 pounds and measuring 11½ feet in length, was caught off Rockport by R. C. Webster on September 1, 1960.

Cod. ISLES OF SHOALS, N.H.: The world's record cod (98 pounds; 5 feet, 3 inches long) was taken in the water of the Isles of Shoals by Alphonse Bielevich on June 8, 1969.

Striper. CUTTYHUNK, MASS.: The world's record striped bass was caught here by Edward J. Kirker on October 10, 1969. It weighed 72 pounds and measured 4 feet, 6½ inches.

Tuna. GALILEE, R.I.: A bluefin tuna caught in the 1951 Atlantic Tuna Tournament here weighed 961 pounds, a U.S. record.

Food & Eating

America's First Chewing Gum. BANGOR, ME.: The Curtis brothers began manufacturing gum here in 1848. They made spruce and paraffin gums. One of the Curtises' most popular paraffin brands was Licorice Lulu.

America's First Lollipops. NEW HAVEN, CONN.: "Lollipops" were first sold by the Bradley–Smith Company of New Haven beginning around 1908.

World's Largest Chocolate Easter Basket Maker. PROVIDENCE, R.I.: Kazarian Brothers on Narragansett Avenue here has been producing their chocolate baskets for years. Harry Kazarian says the genuine chocolate basket "is an all-original item in every respect. We have a small plant and do not expect to get any larger. We sell our total production, all we can make, in New England only."

World's Largest Potato Chip.   GARDNER, MASS.: Mr. and Mrs. David J. Buja of Gardner found a potato chip measuring five by three inches on May 4, 1974. The *Guinness Book of World Records,* which recognizes the chip as the world's largest, doesn't say where Mr. and Mrs. Buja found it.

America's First Lunch Wagon.   PROVIDENCE, R.I.: Walter Scott drove a wagon to Westminster Street here to sell coffee, sandwiches, pies and cakes for the first time in 1872. Lunch wagons, horse drawn, were manufactured commercially in Providence by Ruel B. Jones until 1877.

America's First Popcorn.   PLYMOUTH, MASS.: Quadequina, a brother of the Indian chief Massasoit, contributed popcorn to the Pilgrims' Thanksgiving dinner, February 22, 1630. Quadequina brought several bushels of popcorn in a deerskin bag.

America's Most Famous Cookies.   WHITMAN, MASS.: Toll House Cookies (chocolate chip) originated at the Toll House Inn here, which was founded in 1709.

World's Greatest Amount of Ice Cream Consumed in One Sitting.   NORTH ADAMS, MASS.: On May 2, 1975, Ronald C. Long ate eight pounds of ice cream at Friendly's Ice Cream store here. Long's consumption—which amounted to 51 scoops of ice cream—has earned him a place in the *Guinness Book of World Records.*

Football

First College Football Champs.   NEW HAVEN, CONN.: The first inter-collegiate football championship was won by Yale University in the fall of 1876. The Yale team, captained by Eugene Voy ("Hoby") Baker, '77, triumphed over Columbia, Harvard and Princeton.

World's First Football Dummy.   NEW HAVEN, CONN.: Amos Alonzo Stagg improvised a tackling dummy from an old gymnasium mat at Yale University in 1889.

Nation's First Football Club.   BOSTON, MASS.: The Oneida Football Club was organized in 1862, and took on all comers for the next three years without ever losing a game, or even being scored against.

World's First Football Goal Posts.   CAMBRIDGE, MASS.: The posts were used in a game between Harvard University and McGill, of Montreal, May 14, 1874. This was the first football game ever to have an admission charge for spectators. Proceeds were used to throw a party for the Canadian visitors after the game.

Foreigners

America's First Japanese Immigrant. FAIRHAVEN, MASS.: In 1841 a 15-year-old shipwrecked sailor, Nakahama Manjiro, was rescued here by American sailors and enrolled in school, which he attended for six years. When he finally returned to Japan Manjiro was beaten for having left his country. He survived to become the interpreter for Admiral Peary on his visit to Japan in 1853.

America's First Chinese Students. MONSON, MASS.: In 1847 the Rev. Samuel Robbins Brown, head of the Morrison School in China, brought three Chinese students to study at the Monson Academy. After graduating, one of the three, Yung Wing, entered Yale University, and graduated with a B.A. degree in 1854—the first Chinese to graduate from an American university.

Nation's First Japanese Lawyer. BOSTON, MASS.: Takeo Kikuchi got an LL.B. degree from Boston University on June 5, 1877.

Only American-Born King. CAMBRIDGE, MASS.: The only king born in the U.S. was Bhumibol Adulyadej, King of Thailand. He was born in Mt. Auburn Hospital here in 1927 and ascended the Thai throne in 1950 as King Pama IX.

Assorted Games & Sports

World's Shortest Prizefight.   LEWISTON, ME.: On September 29, 1946, Al Couture knocked out Ralph Walton here in 10½ seconds. This time included a ten-second count. According to the *Guinness Book of World Records,* Couture hit Walton in Walton's corner, having jumped the opening bell.

World's Largest Printer of Play Money.   SALEM, MASS.: Parker Brothers, Inc., prints $18.5 *trillion* worth of Monopoly money each year, more than the annual production by all the world's mints of all the world's currencies.

First Davis Cup Tennis Matches.   BROOKLINE, MASS.: The first tennis matches for the Davis Cup, or International Lawn Tennis Challenge Trophy, were held at the Longwood Cricket Club here in August of 1900. The matches were won by the American team, three matches to none, against England.

Nation's Only Nearsighted Polo Club. HAMILTON, MASS.: Founded exclusively for nearsighted members, the Myopia Hunt Club dates from 1882.

THE BOSTON BRUINS

Most Wins in a Season.   The Bruins' 78-game 1970-1 hockey season had 57 wins, 14 losses and 1 tie, a National Hockey League record. In that season the Bruins scored a record total of 399 goals.

Longest Winning Streak.   The Bruins won fourteen consecutive games in 1929-30, an NHL record.

Most Goals by a Player.   The Bruins' Phil Esposito scored 76 goals in 1970-1, more than any other player in NHL history. Esposito is the only NHL player to have scored 100 or more points in seven different seasons.

Most Assists by a Player.   Bobby Orr of the Bruins has the NHL record—102 goals assisted (1970-1).

America's Only Australian Aborigine-Style Walkabout Trail. GLOCESTER, R.I.: This meandering woods trail, more than eight miles long, was laid out by the officers and men of the Australian destroyer H.M.A.S. *Perth* in 1965 while they were waiting in Rhode Island to take delivery of a newly built ship. The name of the trail refers to the nomadic habits of the Australian aborigines. The trail leads through part of the George Washington State Forest in Glocester.

World's First Volleyball Game. HOLYOKE, MASS.: William George Morgan, physical director of the YMCA, developed the game here in 1895, first calling it Mintonette and using a basketball bladder batted over a rope by hand. A leather-covered ball and eight-foot-high net were adopted later. A YMCA volleyball committee established rules in 1900.

Nation's First Rope Ski Tow. WOODSTOCK, VT.: Robert Royce used 900 yards of rope powered by an old Model T Ford engine to haul skiers up Gilbert's Hill here as early as January 1934. Most ski historians accept the Woodstock tow as America's first, but some feel a similar tow in GILFORD, N.H. antedated it by a year or two. The Gilford rope tow, whenever it began, became notorious for its speed; it pulled at 30 miles per hour. Going up the hill there was almost as risky as coming down.

America's First Chair Lift. STOWE, VT.: A single-chair ski lift was installed here on the slopes of Mt. Mansfield in 1940.

America's First Intercollegiate Billiards Match. WORCESTER, MASS.: On July 25, 1860, Harvard and Yale engaged in a "grand trial of skill." A six-pocket, 6-by-12-foot table, and four balls—one white, one spotted, one pink and one red—were used. Pushing and crotching were allowed. Benjamin Thomas Frothingham and William Stackpole of Harvard won with 800 points against 720 for George St. John Sheffield and Theodore C. Bacon of Yale. The best run was 45, made by Bacon.

Geography

America's Furthest East
WEST QUODDY HEAD, ME.: This is the easternmost point
in the U.S. (longitude 66°, 57′ West).
LUBEC, ME.: This is the easternmost town in the U.S.
EASTPORT, ME.: This is the easternmost city in the U.S.

NEW ENGLAND'S POPULATION

New England's Most Heavily Populated Area. SUFFOLK
COUNTY, MASS.: The population density of Suffolk County,
south of Boston, is 13,128 people per square mile, by far the
highest concentration in New England.

New England's Least Populated Area. PISCATAQUIS
COUNTY, ME.: The population density of Piscataquis County
in north-central Maine is 4 people per square mile. Other New
England counties with similar low densities are Vermont's Essex
with 8 people per square mile, and Maine's Washington with
12.

America's First Globes. BRADFORD, VT.: The first geo-graphic globes produced in the United States came from here, made by James Wilson beginning in 1811. An historical record describes Wilson as an "impoverished farmer," who succeeded in making the globes only after "11 years of study and labor."

America's Largest Outdoor Globe. WELLESLEY, MASS.: The Babson World Globe shows the earth as it would look to a viewer 5,000 miles away in space. It measures 28 feet in diame-ter and weighs 21½ tons. The globe rotates to show night and day.

America's Only Floating Island. WHITINGHAM, VT.: In Lake Sadawga here is a large island which floats on the surface, anchored to the lake floor by the roots of trees which grow on the island. Pieces of the island from time to time break free of the main and float about the lake, hindering boating activities by summer residents on the shore. The island, a dense mat of vegetation and roots, supports 30-foot trees and is about 25 acres square. Lake Sadawga's is the only floating island in the U.S., and, indeed, in the Western Hemisphere (there is another one in a lake in the Swiss Alps).

NEW ENGLAND'S ISLANDS

New England's Largest Island. MOUNT DESERT, ME.: Among U.S.-owned islands in the Atlantic, only Long Island exceeds Mount Desert (108 square miles) in size.

Second Largest Island in New England is Martha's Vineyard, Mass. (91 square miles).

America's Largest U.S. Map. WELLESLEY, MASS.: The Coleman Map is the largest map of the U.S. in the nation. A 3,000-square-foot relief map, it measures 65 feet east to west and 45 feet north to south, and was 17 years in the building.

World's First Map To Bear the Name "America." PROVI-DENCE, R.I.: The name appears on the Waldseemuller Map (1507) in the John Carter Brown Library here.

NEW ENGLAND'S CAVERNS

New England's Biggest Cave. SALISBURY, CONN.: The two caves near the Twin Lakes here, called the Bashful Lady and the Jack-in-the-Pulpit caves, are each about 600 feet long. The Bashful Lady cave is named for a stalactite-stalagmite formation which looks like a woman with her face turned to the cave wall. Other features of this cave include the Blue Bathroom and the Lemon Squeeze. The caves were first discovered during the time of the Civil War by a hunter whose dog had wandered into one of them.

Golf

Nation's First Golf Course. NEWPORT, R.I.: A nine-hole course was completed in 1890 at Benton's Point near here.

Nation's Only Town With Eight Golf Courses. REHOBOTH, MASS.: Rehoboth is called Golf Town, U.S.A. There is a golf course for every 814 Rehobotheans, it turns out—which hardly seems like enough, when you think about it.

World's Largest Golf Green. BOLTON, MASS.: The fifth green at Runaway Brook Golf Course in Bolton has an area of more than 28,000 square feet, and is thought to be the largest green in the world.

World's First Golf Tee. BOSTON, MASS.: The golf tee was invented by George F. Grant of Boston. The year was 1899. Before Grant's breakthrough, golf courses featured small sandboxes located beside the tee area. The golfer took a handful of sand and made a little pyramid to set his ball on for driving.

The Grave

Nation's Only Cemetery Containing Remains of the Ancestors of Four Presidents. WOBURN, MASS.: The Ancient Burying Ground here has relations of Franklin Pierce, James Garfield, Grover Cleveland and Benjamin Harrison.

America's First Cemetery with Family Lots. NEW HAVEN, CONN.: Grove Street Cemetery inaugurated the use of family lots in the U.S. The cemetery was laid out in 1796. It contains the graves of many notables, including that of New England Record-holder Charles Goodyear (see under Inventors).

World's Only Gravestone Marked with a Ghostly Leg. BUCKSPORT, ME.: The mark, in the shape of a woman's leg, is on the gravestone of town founder Jonathan Buck in Buck Cemetery. The legend is that the leg is the mark of a witch who was hanged on Buck's orders in the early 1700's.

Nation's Only Grave of the Unknown Indian. HOPKIN-
TON, MASS.: At Mt. Auburn Cemetery here, the story goes,
for many years residents were surprised to find an Indian grave
decorated each Memorial Day. According to a report, "one citi-
zen secreted himself to watch for the donor, but though he came
earlier each succeeding year the grave was always decorated before he arrived. After the death of an elderly lady, the floral trib-
ute ceased."

America's Only Tomb with a Combination Lock. SOUTH
WINDHAM, ME.: The John Anderson tomb in Smith Cemetery here dates back to 1807. The tomb is fitted with a combination lock like a bank vault. A report says that "the combination
is . . . known by a few, if any, now living persons."

Holidays & Festivals

Nation's Only State To Legalize Christmas. MASSACHU-
SETTS: Christmas was finally made legal in Massachusetts in
1885, having been outlawed since 1659, when a five-shilling fine
was announced for anybody who took the day off.

World's Only Continuing Celebration of VJ Day. RHODE
ISLAND: The state has a VJ Day holiday each August on the
second Monday of the month.

World's Only Evacuation Day. BOSTON, MASS.: The day
British troops withdrew from Boston in 1776 is celebrated on a
day which, fortuitously, coincides with St. Patrick's Day. Evacuation Day, an official holiday in Suffolk County, Mass., was
created to make it possible to close public offices on St. Patrick's
Day without appearing to favor the Irish.

World's Only Annual Bean-Hole Bean Festival. SOUTH PARIS, ME.: Held the last Saturday of July, the Bean Hole Bean Festival is sponsored by the Brown & Morrill Company bean cannery. Homemade bean dishes are featured.

World's Only Johnnycake Festival. USQUEPAUGH, R.I.: The Festival is held in October at Kenyon's Grist Mill here. The featured attraction, johnnycake, is made with corn meal ground at the mill.

America's Only Winter Festival Using Imported Snow (unofficial). NORTHAMPTON, MASS.: The annual Winter Festival opened here in January 1977 with the help of a truckload of snow sent as a gift from the city of Buffalo, New York. A thaw and rain had made it the fifth consecutive Festival on bare ground in Northampton. Boy Scouts who were supposed to unload the snow failed to show up, so Mayor David Cramer and other town officials shoveled it onto the courthouse lawn, where it was given away in bowls under a maple sugar topping.

World's Only Mudbowl Championship. SUGARLOAF MOUNTAIN, ME.: Held in mid-September since 1971, the Mudbowl Festival features a football game played in the mud and the crowning of a Mud Queen.

World's Only Dump Week. KENNEBUNKPORT, ME.: National Dump Week here climaxes with a Trash Parade and the crowning of Miss Dumpy on July 4th. Everyone marches to the town dump.

Hotels

Nation's First First-Class Hotel. BOSTON, MASS.: The Tremont House, which opened on October 16, 1829, had 170 rooms at rates of $2.00 per day (four meals included). An innovation in the hotel was the private single room, for guests who preferred not to double up with others. Other novelties included room keys, free soap, gas lights, and running water in bathrooms in the basement.

America's Most Notorious Example of Architectural Compromise. MONTPELIER, VT.: The old Victorian style Pavilion Hotel (1876) was rebuilt by restoring half of it to its original look and modernizing the other half. It is called the "Epitome of Compromise," and it is used for offices.

America's First Steam-Heated Building. BOSTON, MASS.: The Eastern Hotel, built in 1845, had wrought-iron steam pipes leading to coil radiators. The system was the first steam building heat in the U.S.

Houses

America's First Solar House.   DOVER, MASS.: Built in 1948, the house had a black sheet-metal heat collector behind panes of glass that caught the rays of the sun and stored them in a heat bin, so called, "which worked chemically on a sodium base," according to a report. Electric fans then blew the heat through duct work. This was the first completely sun-heated house in the U.S.

World's Only Wedding Cake House.   KENNEBUNK, ME.: The Wedding Cake House is called "a relic of the scroll-saw era." Ornamented wooden pinnacles rise at the corners, and there is a trellised canopy over the stairs to the front door. Elaborate tracery between the pinnacles gives the effect of a lace net on a Valentine. A sea captain added the decorations to the house to please his bride, who had been deprived of a wedding cake when the captain was abruptly ordered to sea after his wedding.

Only Wedding Cake House.   *Kennebunk, Me.*

America's Oldest Frame House. DEDHAM, MASS.: The Fairbanks House, on Eastern Avenue at the corner of East Street, was built in 1636 by Jonathan Fairbanks. It is now a shrine for 6,000 families named Fairbanks, the builder's descendants. In 1964 a car crashed into the house and destroyed much of its furniture.

World's Only House Made of Newspaper. ROCKPORT, MASS.: Paper House, at Pigeon Cove, is built out of 215 thicknesses of newspaper. Its owner says, "All the furniture is made of newspaper, too, including a desk of newspapers relating to Lindberg's historic flight." The house was built in 1922.

Best House Ever Seen by J. Q. Adams. PROVIDENCE, R.I.: Upon visiting the John Brown house on Power Street in 1789, John Quincy Adams called it "the most magnificent and elegant private mansion that I have ever seen on this continent."

Nation's Greatest Number of Colonial Houses Standing. NEWPORT, R.I.: The town has over 500 Colonial-era dwellings still intact, more than any other town in the U.S.

Individuals

Snowflake King. JERICHO, VT.: W. A. ("Snowflake") Bentley (1865–1952) made 5,300 photographs of snowflakes—no two alike—which are on display here. He took the pictures through a microscope. According to a report "the flakes, caught on a cold board covered with black velvet, were photographed in Bentley's refrigerated camera room." Bentley, a Vermont farmer all his life, is regarded as one of the pioneers of microphotography.

America's First Astronomer. CAMBRIDGE, MASS.: John Winthrop made sunspot observations from here on April 19, 20 and 22, 1739. The 21st was cloudy. Winthrop's reports of his observations, in the Harvard University archives, have never been published.

World's Only Person to Survive Having a Crowbar Blasted Through his Head. RUTLAND, VT.: In 1840 Phineas Gage, in a blasting accident, had a crowbar pierce his head, leaving a three-inch hole. A report says "doctors rushed to the scene, found Gage sitting on a hotel veranda coolly chatting with friends; he recovered fully, died 21 years later in Chile."

World's First Captain to Sail Alone Around the Globe. BOSTON, MASS.: Captain Joshua Slocum, a Canadian, sailed from Boston on April 24, 1895 in the 36-foot sloop, *Spray*. Slocum sailed from Boston to Cape Horn via Gibraltar, then on to Australia. From Australia he sailed to Cape Town, and crossed to the Leeward Islands, completing the last leg of his 46,000-mile voyage in Newport, R.I., on June 27, 1898.

America's Richest Businesswoman. BELLOWS FALLS, VT.: Hetty Robinson Green (1831–1916), "the Witch of Wall Street," was, among businesswomen, the world's richest in eccentricity as well as in wealth. Born in New Bedford, Mass., she moved to Bellows Falls in 1875 when she married a native son. Hetty was thrifty: she wore shabby, dirty old clothes, cut up used newspapers for underwear, instructed her laundry to wash only those parts of her dresses that trailed on the ground—this from a woman who had $750,000 a year and whose personal fortune exceeded $100 million during the last years of her life.

Nation's First and Greatest Mathematical Prodigy. CABOT, VT.: The United States's first and most celebrated mathematical child prodigy was Zerah Colburn, who was born here in 1804. Before he turned seven, Zerah was touring the country solving arithmetical puzzles and complex calculations. In his head, he could raise the number 8 to the sixteenth power, give the square root of 106,929, or the cube root of 268,336,125, all in less time than it took observers to write the numbers down.

Zerah eventually retired from exhibition and returned to Vermont, where he died at 35.

World's Only Telepathic Novelist (unofficial). BRATTLE-BORO, VT.: The only recorded telepathic collaborator of Charles Dickens's was T. P. James, a Brattleboro printer who in 1873 announced the completion of Dickens's *Mystery of Edwin Drood,* which was unfinished when Dickens died in 1870. The "Spirit Pen" of the dead author had in reality finished the novel using T. P. James as a medium, James said. The book sold pretty well.

World's Longest-Lived Triplets. MARLBORO, MASS.: Faith, Hope and Charity Caughlin were born here March 27, 1868 and all lived well over 90 years. First to die was Hope, aged 93.

World's Most Famous Midget. BRIDGEPORT, CONN.: Charles Sherwood Stratton, known as General Tom Thumb, was born here January 11, 1832 and died July 15, 1883. At age 18 Stratton was 30½ inches tall, and at age 30 he had only grown 4½ inches. Stratton kept growing, however: at his death he was three feet four.

Institutions

America's Oldest Country Club. BROOKLINE, MASS.:
Founded in 1882, the Brookline Country Club's grounds extend
over about 100 acres. Facilities available include golf, curling
and steeplechase.

World's Only Retired Pirates' Home. MACHIAS, ME.: In
the early 1700's, Samuel ("Black Sam") Bellamy, Robin Hood
of the High Seas, located a pirate village here—a fortified site
where pirates could live in security with all their wants attended
to. Bellamy was drowned in the course of a piratical expedition
before he could enjoy the results of his vision.

World's Largest Center for Genetics Research on Mammals. BAR HARBOR, ME.: Jackson Laboratory here,
founded in 1929, employs 450 people, including a scientific staff
of 38. Laboratory mice, bred for genetic uniformity, are the
principal research tool of Jackson Labs. Two million mice a
year are born in the laboratories—or more than 6,000 each day.

America's Oldest Active Military Organization. NEW-PORT, R.I.: The Artillery Company of Newport, chartered in 1741, has an armory at 23 Clark Street here with a public display of military uniforms. The Company has served in all the country's wars since its foundation.

Inventions

First United States Patent. PITTSFORD, VT.: The first patent was granted in 1790 here to Samuel Hopkins for a process of manufacturing pot and pearl ashes.

America's First Hair Clippers. WORCESTER, MASS.: George Henry Coates made clippers superior to those imported from England, beginning in 1876.

World's First Folding Theater Chair. BOSTON, MASS.: Aaron H. Allen got a patent for such a chair on December 5, 1854 on "an improvement in seats for public buildings."

First Dress Patterns. STERLING, MASS.: In 1863 Ebenezer Butterick here invented the paper pattern for cutting material to be used in dressmaking.

America's First Self-Winding Clock. LITCHFIELD, CONN.: Benjamin Hanks manufactured a clock for which he applied for a patent in 1783, described as "a clock or machine that winds itself up by help of the air and will continue to do so without any other aid."

World's First Atomic Clock. MALDEN, MASS.: A clock run on atomic power was made by the National Company, Inc., of Malden in 1956. The clock was seven feet high and priced at $50,000.

World's First Annunciator. BOSTON, MASS.: Seth Fuller introduced a system of "hanging bells" in the Tremont House hotel, Boston. There were 140 bells in a space 57 feet long, 6 feet high and 1 foot deep. Each bell corresponded with a room in the hotel. The system was placed in operation when the hotel opened, October 16, 1829.

Nation's First Artificial Legs. MEREDITH, N.H.: Benjamin F. Palmer devised a leg with a pliable noiseless joint that kept its shape in all positions, and patented it in 1846. Nine years earlier, a forerunner of this leg was shown at a show of the Massachusetts Charitable Mechanics Association at Brookfield.

World's First Vulcanization of Rubber. WOBURN, MASS.: Charles Goodyear accidentally invented the process of vulcanization when in 1839 he dropped a ball of latex mixed with sulphur on a hot stove. The burned rubber, Goodyear found, remained pliable in the cold and did not soften in the heat, as earlier rubber had.

World's First Underwater Diving Suit. DIXFIELD, ME.:
Leonard Norcross invented a "water dress" and got a patent on
it in 1834. An airtight rubber suit had a brass helmet attached
to the shoulders. A rubber hose from an air pump aboard a boat
was connected to the helmet. The feet of the suit were weighted
with lead.

World's First Leather Belt Drive. LOWELL, MASS.: Paul
Moody devised a system of leather belts to transmit power from
shaft to shaft for use in the Appleton Cotton Mill here in 1828.
The belts replaced iron gears, which had previously been used
to transmit power.

World's First Blackboard. CONCORD, VT.: A country
schoolteacher, Rev. Samuel Read Hall, invented the blackboard here in 1823.

World's First Alarm Clock. CONCORD, N.H.: The alarm
clock was invented by Levi Hutchens of Concord in 1787. The
original model was 2½ feet high and seems to have been in-
tended for persons of regular habits only: its alarm could not be
set, but went off at the same time each day.

America's First Machine-Made Sewing Needles. WOL-
COTTVILLE, CONN.: The Excelsior Needle Company here
made, beginning in 1866, needles with the "cold swaging process," which produced needles cheaper than the crude handmade
kind sold up to that time.

America's First Metal Roller Skate. SPRINGFIELD, MASS.: Everett Hosmer Barney invented a metal clamp to attach skates to shoes in 1866, making possible the modern roller skate.

World's First Friction Matches. CHICOPEE, MASS.: Daniel M. Chapin and a partner began making matches here in 1834. Some of these first matches are still in the possession of "old Chicopee families," according to a report.

World's First Snowmobile. WEST OSSIPEE, N.H.: V. D. White invented the snowmobile here in 1913. White put caterpillar treads on an old Ford body and ski runners on the front. The inventor used the Snowmobile name for his machine, and produced them from a factory in West Ossipee.

World's First Ball-Point Pen. WEYMOUTH, MASS.: The ball-point was invented by John J. Loud of Weymouth. The ball-point is 90 years old: Loud's patent was awarded on October 30, 1888.

America's First Streetlights. NEWPORT, R.I.: In 1806 David Melville installed the first gas lights on Pelham Street in Newport.

America's First Internal Combustion Engine. ORFORD, N.H.: Captain Samuel Morey patented a "gas or vapor engine" in 1826. It had two cylinders, poppet valves, a carburetor, an electric spark, and water cooling equipment. Morey used as fuel turpentine combined with air. The spirits were made by pouring the turpentine into a tin dish and heating the dish with a table lamp. The engine produced a rotary movement with a flywheel.

World's Only Major Invention To Be Perfected in a Dream. NEW HARTFORD, CONN.: Elias Howe, inventor of the practical sewing machine, was living here at the time he brought the invention to completion (1843). At one point Howe's design lacked only a means of feeding thread to the stitching mechanism. The inventor then dreamed one night that he had been captured by a savage tribe whose chief demanded he produce a workable sewing machine within 24 hours on pain of death. Howe couldn't do it, and was due for execution by spears. As the spears descended upon him he observed *they were pierced with eye-shaped holes at their heads.* Awaking, he realized that the solution to his machine's thread-feed problem was to place the eye holes in the points of the needles.

Tallest Library.   Amherst, Mass.

Libraries

World's Tallest Library.   AMHERST, MASS.: The University of Massachusetts Library opened in May 1973, and stands 296 feet, 4 inches high (28 stories). The *Guinness Book of World Records* recognizes this as the tallest library in the world.

America's First Public Library.   DUBLIN, N.H.: The Juvenile Library, founded here in 1822, was the country's first free library. The library in nearby Peterborough, N.H., was the first library in America to be tax supported.

World's Only Library Hauled Over the Ice on a Lake.   EAST VASSALBORO, ME.: The Vassalboro Public Library was originally a cottage on the opposite side of China Lake from the village. When it was donated to the town for use as a library it was placed on skids and hauled by horses over the ice to its present site.

Machines

America's First Printing Press. MONTPELIER, VT.: The
Stephen Daye Press is on display in the Vermont Historical Society Museum here. The press was brought to America from
England in 1638 and continued in use for nearly 150 years, first
around Boston and later in Vermont.

World's Strongest Steady Magnetic Field. CAMBRIDGE,
MASS.: A magnet at the Francis Bitter National Magnet Laboratory at the Massachusetts Institute of Technology was put
into operation in 1964. It produces a magnetic field of 225,000
gauss using 10 megawatts of power.

World's First Doughnut Hole Machine. THOMASTON,
ME.: John F. Blondel of Thomaston got a patent for this invention in 1872. A spring pushed the dough out of a center tube to
form the hole.

First Printing Press.   *Montpelier, Vt.*

World's Biggest Wind Machine. RUTLAND, VT.: The biggest wind engine in history was built here in 1941 to generate electricity from the top of a hill called Grandpa's Knob. The Smith–Putnam wind turbine was fixed atop a 110-foot tower, weighed 250 tons, and had two 70-foot-long rotor blades. It worked on and off for four years until one of the eight-ton blades flew off one night in a stiff breeze.

America's First File Manufacturing Machine. GREEN-FIELD, MASS.: Morris Belknap invented the machine in 1812. As far as is known, it was not a success.

Nation's First Toothpick Machine. GRANVILLE, MASS.: Silas Noble and James P. Cooley patented a machine in 1872 that would permit "a block of wood, with little waste, at one operation, to be cut up into toothpicks ready for use."

America's First Practical Typewriter. NORWICH, CONN.: Charles Thurber invented the Chirographer in 1843, calling it Thurber's Patent Printer, and proposing it as an aid for the blind. An inking roller was used. Thurber's machine "lacked speed," according to Kane's *Famous First Facts*.

America's First Rock Crusher. NEW HAVEN, CONN.: Eli Whitney Blake patented "an improvement in machines for crushing stones" in 1858. Blake's machine chewed the rocks up between steel jaws, one movable and the other fixed.

Largest Wind Machine.   Rutland, Vt.

World's First Sewing Machine to Sew Curving Seams. WA-
TERTOWN, CONN.: Allen Benjamin Wilson patented in 1854
the famous Four-Motion Feed, which made a curved seam possible on a machine for the first time.

World's Most Powerful Forging Press. NORTH GRAF-
TON, MASS.: A Loewy Forging Press at the Wyman–Gordon
Company here is 114 feet, 2 inches high and weighs 10,600 tons.
In use since 1955, the machine's forging capacity is 50,000 tons.

America's First Pointed Screw Machine. PROVIDENCE,
R.I.: Cullen Whipple invented a machine to make pointed
screws and patented it in 1856. Before this, the threaded ends of
screws were blunt, and holes had to be drilled before they could
be used.

The Mail

America's First Postage Stamps.   BRATTLEBORO, VT.: In 1845 the Brattleboro postmaster issued 400 five-cent stamps for use by the Brattleboro post office, anticipating the rest of the country by one year. Brattleboro stamps sell for $12,000 apiece today.

America's First International Dog Sled Mail.   LEWISTON, ME.: Alden William Pulsifer, postmaster of Minot, Me., took a load of mail out of Lewiston on December 20, 1928, on a regular eight-foot mushing sled weighing 200 pounds and pulled by six blackhead Eskimo dogs. Pulsifer averaged nine miles per hour and made 40 to 60 miles per day. The mail pouch was delivered at Montreal on January 14, 1929. The sled returned to Lewiston on February 2, after passing through four states and provinces and 118 cities, covering 600 miles—of which ninety percent was barren of snow.

America's First Post Office Building.   NEWPORT, R.I.: The Custom House and Post Office here, finished in 1830, was the first building built as a post office in the U.S.

World's Largest Stamp Dealer. BOSTON, MASS.: H. E. Harris and Company, on Summer Street here, is the world's biggest vendor of postage stamps, trading in millions of stamps from all nations each year. The firm was founded in 1916 by Henry Ellis Harris, who was then only 18. Today the company employs about 360 people.

World's First Postage Meter. STAMFORD, CONN.: The first postage meter, manufactured by the Pitney Bowes Company here, was put into service on November 16, 1920—the birthdate of metered mail, and a black day for stamp collectors everywhere.

Medicine

World's First Use of Laughing Gas as an Anesthetic. HART-FORD, CONN.: On December 11, 1844, Dr. Horace Wells, a dentist, had one of his teeth pulled under a nitrous oxide (laughing gas) anesthetic administered here by another dentist, Dr. John M. Riggs. The use of the gas was not successful, as Wells did not know it had to be combined with oxygen, a discovery which was not made until 24 years later.

America's First Smallpox Vaccination. BROOKLINE, MASS.: In 1721 Dr. Zabdiel Boylston inoculated his son and two slaves. He succeeded in preventing smallpox in these three, thus helping to overcome widespread fear of vaccination as a medical treatment.

First Successful Peritonitis Preventative. BOSTON, MASS.: Dr. Herbert Lester Johnson in 1922 used amniotic fluid to prevent postoperative peritonitis. The first fluid Johnson used came from caesarean operations on humans. Later a commercial product was made from bovine fluid.

Nation's First Artificial Impregnation. WORCESTER, MASS.: Dr. Gregory Pincus of Clark University here produced a rabbit in 1939 by removing an egg from the ovum of a female rabbit and fertilizing it in a test tube. The egg was then transferred to the uterus of a second rabbit which acted as an incubator.

World's First Medicated Plaster. DEDHAM, MASS.: Dr. John Parker Maynard dissolved gun cotton in sulphuric ether to obtain a fluid to be applied to the skin and covered with cotton strips. He announced the discovery on March 27, 1848.

Nation's First Chiropodist. BOSTON, MASS.: Nehemiah Kenison opened an office on Washington Street across from the Old South Church here in 1840 where he developed instruments and dressings for the relief of corns.

First Phrenology in America. BOSTON, MASS.: Phrenology was introduced in America in 1832 when Dr. Johann Gaspar Spurzheim, a distinguished German practitioner, arrived in Boston for a series of lectures on Phrenology. Spurzheim later lectured in Cambridge.

Nation's First Compulsory Health Insurance. NEWPORT, R.I.: The town fathers of Newport decreed in 1734 that sixpence per month be deducted from all seamen as hospital money to release the town from the great expense of supporting sick and wounded seamen.

America's First Polio Epidemic. RUTLAND, VT.: In the summer of 1894 there were 123 cases of poliomyelitis in the area of Rutland and nearby Wallingford, making the first epidemic of this disease on record for the U.S.

America's First Smallpox Epidemic. BOSTON, MASS.: An epidemic struck in and around Boston in May 1721 which carried off twelve to twenty-four percent of the population in the area. Earlier epidemics had decimated the local Indian tribes, but only vague records of them exist.

America's First Patent Medicine Advertisement. BOSTON, MASS.: An ad in the *Boston Almanack* for 1692, inserted by Benjamin Harris and John Allen, announced: "That Excellent Antidote against all manner of Gripings called Aqua anti torminales, which if timely taken, it not only cures the Griping of the Guts, and the Wind Cholick; but preventeth that woful Distemper of the Dry Belly Ach; With printed directions for the use of it. Sold by Benjamin Harris at the London-Coffee House in Boston. Price three shillings the half pint bottle."

Mining

Nation's First Mica Extraction. GRAFTON, N.H.: Mica was first taken from the Ruggles mine in Isinglass Mountain here in 1803.

NEW ENGLAND'S GOLD

New England's Gold Rush. PLYMOUTH, VT.: In 1851, a disappointed Forty-Niner, who had returned to Plymouth from California, where he had failed to strike it rich, discovered gold in Buffalo Brook here. For the next 40 years gold miners panned, sluiced, dredged and tunneled around the brook (re-named Gold Brook). A mining company formed in the 1880's claimed to have extracted more than $2,000 per day from its Plymouth diggings. While the mining company's reports were probably exaggerated, there was undoubtedly gold in the region. People still pan for it in the stream—which is still called Gold Brook.

World's Largest Granite Quarry.   BARRE, VT.: At the Rock of Ages Quarry, two miles south of Montpelier at Graniteville, there are free self-guided tours through a quarry eight miles long and three miles wide. The granite deposit goes down into the earth an estimated ten miles.

Monuments

World's Only Monument to a Haystack. WILLIAMS-
TOWN, MASS.: The Haystack Monument in Mission Park
here marks the spot where six Williams College students met in
1806 to found the American Board of Foreign Missions. A rainstorm blew up while the six were meeting, and they sheltered
under a nearby haystack.

World's Only Monument to a Wolf Fight. ABINGTON,
CONN.: Wolf Den State Park here has a plaque marking the
cave where the Revolutionary General Israel Putnam
(1718–1790) in his youth fought and killed the last wolf in
Connecticut.

America's Only Monument to a Chicken. ADAMSVILLE,
R.I.: The Rhode Island Red Monument is on the village common. A pointed granite stone marks the spot where the famous
breed of fowl originated.

World's Only Monument to Ether.   BOSTON, MASS.: The Ether Monument in the Public Garden here (1867) commemorates the introduction, by William Thomas Green Morton, of ether as an anesthetic. In 1846, ether was first used at the Massachusetts General Hospital to anesthetize a surgical patient.

Mountains

Nation's Highest Point on the Atlantic Coast. CADILLAC
MOUNTAIN, ME.: The summit, at 1,532 feet, is the highest
point on the coast north of Rio de Janeiro.

NEW ENGLAND'S HIGHEST

New England's Highest Point. MT. WASHINGTON, N.H.:
The summit (6,288 feet) is the highest point in New England,
and the third highest point in the eastern U.S.

New England's Second Highest Point is Mt. Katahdin in
Maine (see below), and its **Third Highest** is Vermont's Mt.
Mansfield (4,393 feet).

**America's Only Mountain To Be the Subject of a Dedication
by a Major Novelist.** MT. GREYLOCK, MASS.: In 1852
Herman Melville, then living in Pittsfield, Mass., dedicated his
seventh novel, *Pierre, or The Ambiguities,* to nearby Mt. Greylock.

It was the custom among earlier authors to dedicate their works to "Majesty," Melville wrote, and so he was dedicating his to the majestic mountain, at 3,491 feet the highest point in Massachusetts. At the time, Melville had just finished *Moby Dick*.

First Land in U.S. To Get the Morning Sun.   MT. KATAHDIN, ME.: The summit, at 5,269 feet, is the highest in Maine, and its eastern face receives direct radiation from the rising sun before any other point in the U.S.

Museums

World's Only Nut Museum.   OLD LYME, CONN.: Elizabeth Tashjian, who runs the Nut Museum here, says, "Nuts have been talking to me for a long time." Admission to the museum is one nut. The world's largest nutcracker, eight feet long, guards the entrance to the nineteenth-century mansion housing the collection of some 50 species of nuts. Of Armenian descent, Miss Tashjian wears an Armenian robe of her grandmother's as a reminder, she says, "that most popular nuts come from Asia Minor." The museum has nut masks, nut paintings done by the museum owner, and the world's largest nut, weighing 35 lbs.

America's Only Lock Museum.   TERRYVILLE, CONN.: The Lock Museum of America on Main Street here has 18,000 locks and keys from the nineteenth century, most of them made in Terryville, the Lock Capital of America. Included in the collection is what is thought to be the **World's Largest Padlock,** a dinner-plate-size giant weighing 29 pounds, and also the **World's Smallest Padlock,** a minuscule earring lock.

Only Postcard Museum.   Canaan, Conn.

World's Only Postcard Museum.   CANAAN, CONN.: Ruth
McCallum's Post Card Museum, appropriately located near the
post office here, displays over 6,000 cards published all over the
world between 1900 and 1910. The collection is the result of a

hobby of Mrs. McCallum and her late husband. The cards, arranged on posters, take up two large rooms of an old barn.

America's Only Fly Fishing Museum. MANCHESTER, VT.: The American Museum of Fly Fishing is operated by the Orvis Company here. There is also a fly fishing school at the museum. Orvis, by the way, manufactures the **World's Only Silk Longjohns:** "warmth without clumsiness."

Nation's First Paper Museum. CAMBRIDGE, MASS.: The Dard Hunter Paper Museum at the Massachusetts Institute of Technology opened in 1939. Hunter, its curator, spent 40 years collecting papers from every paper-making country on earth.

America's Largest Exhibition of Ancient Japanese Armor. LACONIA, N.H.: The Million Dollar Show, founded in 1951, has Japanese armor and saddles, and medieval European items.

World's Only Shoe Museum. BOSTON, MASS.: The United Shoe Machinery Corporation at 140 Federal Street has exhibits which include a collection of 1,500 pairs of shoes of all ages (including ancient Egyptian, 2000 B.C.), styles and sizes.

World's Largest Uniform Button Museum. SOUTHINGTON, CONN.: The museum, called Just Buttons, in an eighteenth-century house here, has thousands of buttons dating back three centuries.

America's Only Exhibit of Glass Flowers. CAMBRIDGE, MASS.: In the Harvard University Museum on Oxford Street, according to a guidebook, "models of the humbler flowers of field and wood are realistically reproduced with an astonishing delicacy of detail and complete botanic accuracy. The secret of this art was discovered in the nineteenth century by a German family named Blaschka, and it remains with them."

America's Only Marble Museum. PROCTOR, VT.: In addition to the Museum, the Vermont Marble Company provides a pile of pieces of marble which visitors may pick through. The town has marble sidewalks, a marble bridge, and a marble high school.

Nation's Only Cartoon Hall of Fame. GREENWICH, CONN.: The Museum of Cartoon Art and Hall of Fame has a collection of works from the period of Thomas Nast and Charles Dana Gibson to the present.

Music

Nation's Only State Song Composed on Top of a Barn. SUTTON, N.H.: The song "Autumn in New Hampshire," which in 1977 was made the fourth official state song by the legislature, was composed in 1956 by Leo H. Austin while he was roofing his barn in Sutton. Mr. Austin is an Irish tenor. His wife says, "We were both on the roof when he was inspired, so I rushed down to find something to write [the song] on. I think it was a brown paper bag." The Austins' daughter, Barbara Ann Patriquin of Chester, N.H., first sang the song at a Knights of Columbus Bicentennial musical program in Manchester, N.H. She had also made a recording of it.

World's First Singing of the Song "America." BOSTON, MASS.: On July 4, 1832, school children here sang this song in the Park Street Church. The song had been written in half an hour on a scrap of paper by Dr. Samuel Francis Smith at the church. The manuscript of the lyrics is in the Harvard University library.

Nation's First Singing Contest.   DORCHESTER, MASS.: A contest was held in 1790 between the singers of the Dorchester First Parish and the Singing Society of Stoughton. The Stoughtonians started off with "Heavenly Vision," the composition of Jacob French, one of their members. They finally sang the Hallelujah Chorus from Handel's "Messiah." This last was sung without any printed music whatever, and to such effect that, according to a report, "the Dorchesterians gave up the contest and gracefully acknowledged defeat."

World's Largest Choir.   BOSTON, MASS.: A choir of 20,000 voices, conducted by Johann Strauss the younger, sang at the World Peace Jubilee here on June 17, 1872. An orchestra playing with the choir numbered 2,000 musicians.

World's Only Version of "The Star Spangled Banner" that Is Easy To Sing.   WEST HARTFORD, CONN.: Music teacher Frank Caruso, 82, has copyrighted a special version of the National Anthem with a narrow vocal range. Mr. Caruso's arrangement lowers the high note from F to middle C and raises the low notes an octave. He claims that seven out of eight people cannot sing all the notes of the National Anthem in its unaltered form. Mr. Caruso has written the following wire to President Carter: "Dear Mr. President: Millions of United States citizens want to enjoy singing our National Anthem. Please help them."

World's First Silent Music.   MIDDLETOWN, CONN.: A work by composer John Cage entitled "Four Minutes Thirty-three Seconds" is completely silent throughout its entirety. First performed here in 1952, the composition consisted of three movements, all perfectly soundless.

Musical Instruments

America's First Melodeon. CONCORD, N.H.: C. Austin patented a melodeon in 1849. It was a small reed organ with a bellows worked by treadles that sucked air through the reeds.

World's First Steam Calliope. WORCESTER, MASS.: The Steam Piano, as it was called, was invented here by Joshua Stoddard in 1855.

America's Second Largest Pipe Organ. PORTLAND, ME.: The Kotzchmar Memorial Organ in Municipal Auditorium here was placed in memory of Herman Kotzchmar, a beloved local organist and composer. It is said to be eight instruments in one, with 177 speaking stops and couplers, 6,500 pipes, and a carillon. Concerts are given here in the summer by members of the American Guild of Organists. In America, the Kotzchmar is exceeded in size only by the Auditorium Organ in Atlantic City, N.J. (the world's largest musical instrument according to the *Guinness Book of World Records*).

America's First Carillon. BOSTON, MASS.: In 1744 Thomas Gunter guaranteed payment for eight bells ordered from Abell Rudhall's foundry in Gloucester, England. Priced at 560 pounds sterling, the bells were installed in Boston's Old North Church in 1745.

America's First Player Piano. CAMBRIDGE, MASS.: John McTammany, Jr., patented a mechanical musical instrument in 1881 for the automatic playing of organs, Narrow sheets of flexible perforated paper governed notes to be played.

America's Largest and Heaviest Paul Revere Bell. PROVI-DENCE, R.I.: The bell, cast by Revere's foundry, was placed in the steeple of the First Congregational Church on Benefit Street here in 1816. The church is now known as the First Unitarian Church of Providence. The bell, originally cast in England, was re-cast by Paul Revere and his son at their foundry in Canton, Mass. It weighs 2,488 lbs., is 36 inches tall, and 12 feet, 11 inches in circumference.

Newspapers

America's Oldest Newspaper. HARTFORD, CONN.: The *Hartford Courant* began publishing in 1764.

America's Only Panther Editor (unofficial). RUTLAND, VT.: The Rutland *Herald* reportedly has a special editor to deal with the many reports of local sightings of panthers, also called cougars or pumas, although the last one proved to exist in New England was shot in the town of Barnard, Vermont, in 1881.

America's First College Daily Newspaper. NEW HAVEN, CONN.: The *Yale Daily News* was first published in 1878 by the students of Yale College. Today the Yalie Daily boasts a circulation of 3,500.

World's Largest Newspaper Page. NANTUCKET, MASS.: The *Nantucket Inquirer & Mirror* has a page size of 30 by 22 inches (660 square inches). *The New York Times,* by comparison, has a page size of only 14½ by 23 inches (333½ square inches).

Paper Products

America's First Gummed Labels. FRAMINGHAM, MASS.: In 1901 the Dennison Company produced the first gummed labels. The firm is also the nation's largest manufacturer of crepe paper.

World's Toughest Paper. DALTON, MASS.: The Crane Paper Mills here manufactures a liner sheet that can be folded 40 times in one place without tearing. Crane makes the sheet for the U.S. Government, which prints money on it. The company has supplied paper for U.S. currency since 1846.

World's First Square-Bottomed Paper Bag. WEST DENNIS, MASS.: Luther C. Crowell of West Dennis gave the world the modern paper bag in 1872, and a machine to make it.

World's First Window Envelope. SPRINGFIELD, MASS.: The U.S. Envelope Company first manufactured this item in 1902 after leasing a patent taken out by Americus F. Callahan.

America's First Blotting Paper.   NEW HAVEN, CONN.: Joseph Parker & Son Company made blotting paper at the West Rock Paper Mill here in 1856 on a Fourdrinier machine.

America's First Paper Twine Machine. WORCESTER, MASS.: In 1895 George Loomis Brownell invented a patented machine that twisted ribbons of paper into cord that, at $1/_{1,000}$-inch thickness was as strong as any known steel of the same gauge.

Politics & Politicians

America's Largest State Legislative Body. CONCORD, N.H.: The New Hampshire legislature's membership varies between 375 and 400. It is the third largest legislative body in the world; the British Parliament and the United States Congress are bigger.

Footloose Legislator. FAIR HAVEN, VT.: Matthew Lyon (1750–1822), elected to the United States Congress from Vermont in 1797, is the only man known to have served in Congress from three different states. Having left Vermont, he was sent to Washington from Kentucky and later from Arkansas.

First Brother Governors. BOSTON, MASS.: The first brothers to serve simultaneously as state governors were Levi Lincoln, who was governor of Massachusetts from 1825–1834, and his brother Enoch, who was governor of Maine from 1827–1829.

America's First Constitution. HARTFORD, CONN.: The "fundamental orders," drafted in 1638 as the instrument of government for the new Connecticut colony, were the first constitution in the Americas.

Most Fastidious Legislator. CALAIS, VT.: Pardon James (1788–1870) of Calais had a touching phobia, and wore a short pitchfork strapped to his arm so he need not touch any object handled by other human beings. He represented Calais in the state legislature from 1828 to 1831.

Jailhouse Congressman. FAIR HAVEN, VT.: Matthew Lyon of Fair Haven, a collector of more than one New England record (see **Footloose Legislator**) became the first Congressman to do time. He was jailed in 1798 for a violation of the Sedition Act during the so called "Federalist Reign of Terror." Lyon served four months and was fined $1,000. He was re-elected to Congress while in prison. Lyon's fine was posthumously refunded (to his heirs) in 1840.

America's Closest Senate Race. NEW HAMPSHIRE: The 1974 contest between Louis Wyman, a Republican Congressman, and John Durkin, a Democrat, for election to the Senate from New Hampshire was the closest in the nation's history. Wyman was originally named victor by 548 votes. The votes were counted again. Durkin came out ahead by ten. Contested ballots were counted. Wyman had 110,926 votes, Durkin 110,924—a two-vote difference. Durkin appealed to the Senate elections committee, which refused to seat either candidate. A new election was ordered, which Durkin won. He was sworn in in September 1975.

Presidents

First Presidential Phone Call. ROCKY POINT, R.I.: The first telephone call made by a U.S. President was placed from Rocky Point to Providence in 1877 by President Rutherford B. Hayes.

First Presidential Car Ride. HARTFORD, CONN.: The first automobile ride by a U.S. President took place here on August 22, 1902, when President Theodore Roosevelt, in a Columbia Electric Victoria, purple lined, led a parade tour of the city.

NEW ENGLAND'S PRESIDENTS

Six presidents of the United States have been New Englanders: John Adams, John Q. Adams and John F. Kennedy from Massachusetts; Chester Arthur and Calvin Coolidge from Vermont; and Franklin Pierce from New Hampshire. In addition, seven presidents besides these have had New England ancestry: Lincoln, Garfield, Benjamin Harrison, Cleveland and Franklin D. Roosevelt (Massachusetts ancestors); Taft and Hayes (Vermont ancestors).

Racing

First Horse to Pace a Mile in Under Two Minutes. READVILLE, MASS.: On August 28, 1897, Star Pointer paced a mile in harness in 1 minute, 59¼ seconds, the first U.S. pacer to break 2 minutes.

First Horse to Trot a Mile in Under Two Minutes. READVILLE, MASS.: On August 24, 1903, the trotter Lou Dillon, with a pacemaker in front, and driven by Millard F. Sanders, made a mile in 1 minute, 58½ seconds, the first U.S. trotter to break 2 minutes.

America's First 300-Mile Horse Race. BURLINGTON, VT.: Ramela, a horse owned by W. R. Brown, president of the Arab Club, won a race from Fort Ethan Allen in Burlington to Camp Devens, Mass., covering the distance in 51 hours, 26½ minutes. The date was October 15, 1919. Ramela was ridden by jockey Albert W. Harris. There were 14 starters in the race, and points were made by ratings of condition of horse, food consumption and daily timing. Every entrant had to cover at least 60 miles a day, and had to be ridden at least 10 hours each day, but no more than 15 hours. Jockey weights ranged from 200 to 245 pounds, according to a report, putting the riders in this race in contention for the **World's Fattest Jockeys (unofficial)** record.

Radio

Nation's First Radio Program Broadcast. BRANT ROCK, MASS.: Prof. Reginald Aubrey Fessenden broadcast the CQ call, followed by a song, the reading of a verse, a violin solo, a speech, and an invitation to report on reception, on the night before Christmas, 1906. The professor's radio was powered by a steam engine. He had set up an antenna 429 feet high.

America's First Transatlantic Wireless (Radio) Station. WELLFLEET, MASS.: Guglielmo Marconi, inventor of wireless telegraphy, erected the tower here and put it into operation in 1901. The first American non-experimental transatlantic broadcast was beamed from here in 1903, when King George VII of England and President Theodore Roosevelt exchanged greetings.

America's First Hotel With Two-Channel Radio Reception. BOSTON, MASS.: The Hotel Statler began broadcasting free programs from a central control room on May 10, 1927. Each of the Statler's 1,300 rooms had individual headsets. Loudspeakers replaced them later.

America's First Radio Church.   PORTLAND, ME.: The Reverend Howard Oliver Hough established the Radio Parish Church of America in a broadcast from the studio of WCSH here on April 18, 1926, in a room of the Congress Square Hotel. Nine denominations were represented in the radio church.

Railroads

Nation's First Railway Accident. QUINCY, MASS.: The Granite Railway, an early line used to transport granite from a quarry to dockside in Quincy, used an inclined plane to draw heavy blocks of stone up into the cars. On July 25, 1832, four visitors were invited to ride up this inclined plane in one of the cars. A chain snapped, and they were thrown over a cliff 40 feet to the ground below. One of the passengers was killed and the others were injured.

America's First Municipal Subway. BOSTON, MASS.: The Tremont Street Subway opened for passenger traffic on September 1, 1897 and was continued to North Station the next year. It was the first shallow subway built below street level—as distinct from a deep tunnel subway.

World's First Cog Railway. MT. WASHINGTON, N.H.: The Mt. Washington Cog Railway, which runs to the peak's

First Cog Railway.   Mt. Washington, N.H.

summit, was invented and built by Sylvester Marsh of Littleton, N.H., in 1866, to be completed in 1869 at a cost of $139,500. The railway, still very much in operation, is one of the East's great tourist attractions.

World's Only Semi-Precious Railroad Station (unofficial). WEST MEDFORD, MASS.: The station, "a bizarre structure built about 1880," was distinguished by semi-precious jewels and other curious objects, including a whale's tooth. These were imbedded in the station's walls at the time it was built. Most of the jewels have been picked out of the cement by souvenir hunters.

Rain-Making, Etc.

America's First Manmade Snow. MT. GREYLOCK, MASS.: Vincent Joseph Schaefer of the General Electric Company scattered pellets of dry ice from a small plane over a path three miles long at an altitude of 14,000 feet here on November 13, 1946. This caused snow to fall from the clouds he passed through. The snow fell for 3,000 feet, but evaporated before reaching the ground.

First U.S. Forest Fire Fought with Manmade Rain. CONCORD, N.H.: An attempt to quench a forest fire near Concord with rain produced by seeding clouds was made on October 29, 1947. Dry ice was dropped into clouds from aircraft. The seeding caused rain to fall, but shortly after the rain-making attempt a natural rainstorm began, so it was impossible to determine the amount of manmade rain produced.

America's First Manmade Lightning. PITTSFIELD, MASS.: The General Electric Company demonstrated a ten million-volt bolt of manmade lightning on June 10, 1932. The previous record had been five million volts. In 1935, GE built the country's **First Lightning Observatory** on the roof of their Pittsfield plant. In a circular form 14 feet in diameter the observatory held a seven-foot-square lightproof room equipped with a periscope with a brilliantly silvered reflecting surface that made lightning flashes from any direction visible in an angled mirror. A motor-operated high-speed camera with 12 lenses recorded lightning on moving strips of film.

Recreation

America's First Roller Coaster.   ARLINGTON, MASS.: The roller coaster was invented in 1898 by Edwin Prescott of Arlington. Three years later Prescott patented a Loop the Loop Centrifugal Railway which had a 70-foot incline and a 20-foot-wide loop.

Nation's First Municipal Bathhouses. BOSTON, MASS.: The L Street Baths were built in 1865 and were maintained under the supervision of the Board of Bath Commissioners.

America's Oldest Park.   BOSTON, MASS.: Boston Common was laid out by John Winthrop (1588–1649), Governor of the Massachusetts Bay Colony, as a cow pasture and training field.

America's First Playground.   BOSTON, MASS.: Three piles of yellow sand were placed at the Children's Mission in 1886 for use as a children's playground—the nation's first.

Nation's First Roller Skating Rink.   NEWPORT, R.I.: James
Leonard Plimpton, inventor of the Plimpton Roller Skate,
opened a rink in 1866 in the Atlantic House at Bellevue Avenue
and Pelham Street.

Nation's Only Vacation Community for Horses. ME-
THUEN, MASS.: A farm given to the Massachusetts Society
for the Prevention of Cruelty to Animals invites race horses to
recuperate here between seasons, or dray horses to rest from
years of labor. It is thought to be the only horse resort in the
U.S.

Religion

World's First Christian Science Church. BOSTON, MASS.:
The Church of Christ, Scientist was organized here in 1879 by
Mary Baker Eddy. The first church building is the granite
structure on Huntington Avenue, built in 1894.

World's First Seventh-Day Adventists. WASHINGTON,
N.H.: The Seventh-Day Adventist Church was founded here as
the First Christian Society in 1842. The sect began to keep the
seventh day as sabbath in 1844.

America's First Holy Rollers. HARDWICK, VT.: In the
1830's an extreme sect called the New Lights sprang up in
Hardwick. The New Lights went in for a "demonstrative cere-
mony," according to a report, in which members rolled around
on the floor—hence "Holy Rollers." The local Congregationalists finally made Hardwick too hot to hold the Rollers, and they
dispersed.

America's First Black Bishop. PORTLAND, ME.: James
Healy was consecrated as bishop of Portland in 1875, having
been ordained a priest in Paris, Me., in 1854.

Rocks & Stones

America's Biggest Drum Rock.   WARWICK, R.I.: Balanced on a ledge on Drum Rock Lane here is a boulder that could at one time be rocked back and forth so as to make a sound audible for a mile. The Drum Rock was a meeting place for Coweset and Narragansett Indians. The boulder is still there, but can no longer be rocked.

America's Biggest Balanced Rock. NEW MARL-BOROUGH, MASS.: A 40-ton boulder here is so delicately balanced that the pressure of a hand will sway but not dislodge it. Called Tipping Rock, it is about half a mile southwest of Southfield.

World's Only Rock on Which the Lord's Prayer Is Carved.   BRISTOL, VT.: On a hill near the village is a large boulder—Prayer Rock—on which the Lord's Prayer was carved on order of a Buffalo, New York, physician. The object, according to a historical report, was "to deter rough teamsters coming up the hill from using profanity." The teamsters would see the Prayer carved in the stone and subdue their language, it was hoped.

Schools & Colleges

World's Largest Private University. BOSTON, MASS.: Northeastern University, with about 34,000 students, is the largest private university in the world.

America's Oldest Public School. BOSTON, MASS.: Boston Latin School opened in 1635 and still thrives. Its full name was the Boston Public Latin School, and its support originally came from voluntary contributions. Boston Latin was founded to instruct pupils in ancient languages so they could study the Bible in the original.

America's Youngest College Graduate. NEW HAVEN, CONN.: Merrill K. Wolf of Cleveland graduated from Yale University with a B.A. in Music in 1945 at the age of 14.

First Girls' Gym at a U.S. College. SOUTH HADLEY, MASS.: Mt. Holyoke College in 1862 gave an optional course in gymnastics in a storeroom over a wood and coal shed. Calisthenics had been given here as early as 1835. By 1865 a separate gymnasium building was erected.

World's Only Girls' School Founded as a Result of the Chance Sighting of a Mother and Two Daughters Braiding Hats. NORTHFIELD, MASS.: The Rev. Dwight L. Moody founded the Northfield School for Girls in 1879. A report says "Moody had been impressed with the hopelessness of girls from poorer homes after driving past a mountain cottage where a mother and two daughters were braiding palmetto straw hats to support a family whose father was a paralytic. All students help with the housework."

Nation's First Reform School. WESTBORO, MASS.: The state reformatory for boys was opened April 9, 1847.

America's First Law School. LITCHFIELD, CONN.: Judge Tapping Reeve opened a law school here in 1784. Ten to twenty students were enrolled. Judge Reeve continued the Litchfield Law School, unaided, for 14 years.

Nation's First Swimming School. BOSTON, MASS.: A school opened at the Mill Dam on July 23, 1827. According to a contemporary account, "A belt is placed around the bodies, under the arms, and attached to a rope and pole, by which the head and body are kept in the proper position in the water, while the pupil is learning the use of his limbs."

Ships & Boats

World's First Steamboat. FAIRLEE, VT.: Inventor Samuel
Morey ran the *Aunt Sally* on the Connecticut River here in 1793,
fourteen years before Robert Fulton launched his *Clermont.*
Morey's craft was described as being "barely large enough to
hold himself, the rude machinery connected with his steam
boiler, and an armful of firewood." Morey also patented an
early internal combustion engine in 1826 (*see* Miscellaneous Inventions). Morey's steamboat never received the recognition it
deserved, a fact which discouraged the inventor to the point
that he sunk his boat in a lake in Fairlee.

America's Oldest Continuously Operating Ferry. GLAS-
TONBURY, CONN.: The ferry to Rocky Hill has been running since 1655. Fare is 25 cents for car and driver, 5 cents for
passengers.

World's Biggest Model Ship. NEW BEDFORD, MASS.: The
Lagoda, a half-scale, full-rigged whaling ship model, occupies a

Biggest Model Ship.   New Bedford, Mass.

room at the Whaling Museum here. Built in 1915 by ship-wrights still skilled in the construction of whalers, the square-rigger measures 89 feet in length.

World's Only Ventilator Cowl Salvaged from the Battleship Maine. WOBURN, MASS.: The U.S.S. *Maine* was blown up in Havana Harbor in 1898, in an incident that touched off the Spanish–American War. The salvaged cowl, a memorial, is on Horn Pond Mountain in Woburn.

World's First Atomic Submarine. GROTON, CONN.: *Nautilus,* the first submarine driven by nuclear power, was built here for the U.S. Navy by General Dynamics Corp. and launched on January 2, 1954.

First Ships To Carry the American Flag Around the World. BOSTON, MASS.: The 212-ton *Columbia* sailed from Boston September 30, 1787, under Captain Kendrick, accompanied by the sloop *Washington* under Captain Robert Gray. They sailed for three years and covered 41,899 miles. The two Boston ships discovered the Straits of Juan de Fuca and the mouth of the Columbia River in the Pacific Northwest. They returned to Boston on August 9, 1790.

America's First Catamaran. PROVIDENCE, R.I.: Nathanael Greene Herreshoff patented a parallel hulled boat for use by lifeguards at beaches on April 20, 1877.

Societies & Groups

World's Only Society for the Protection of Clothes-lines. WALPOLE, N.H.: Founded in 1816 as the Walpole Society for Bringing to Justice Horse Thieves and Pilferers, the organization in 1880 extended the scope of its activities to protecting henroosts and clotheslines. It survives as a social club.

America's First Boy's Camp. MILFORD, CONN.: Frederick William Gunn, who founded the Gunnery School, took 50 boys on a two-week camping trip to Milford in 1861, and again in 1863 and 1865. In 1867 Gunn started a second camp at Point Beautiful on Lake Waramaug, Washington, Conn. These were the first summer camps in this country.

World's First Campfire Girls. LAKE SEBAGO, ME.: Mrs. Luther Halsey Gulick organized the group at her camp here on March 17, 1912. The Campfire Girl motto, "Wohelo," comes from the first two letters of each of the words *work, health* and *love.*

World's Only Holstein-Friesian Association. BRATTLE-BORO, VT.: Founded in 1885, the association, which registers dairy cattle of the Holstein–Friesian breed all over the world, is only one of three cattle breed organizations in New England, **America's Cattle Society Capital.** Farmington, Conn., has the Guernsey Cattle Club; Newport, R.I., has the American Jersey Club.

America's Only Society for Royal Bastards. LAKESIDE, CONN.: The Descendants of the Illegitimate Sons and Daughters of the Kings of England has its U.S. headquarters here. Founded in 1950, the society, which is also called the Royal Bastards, has 125 members. Membership is limited to those who can prove descent from an illegitimate child of British royalty: other bastards need not apply.

The States

Lowest State Taxes. NEW HAMPSHIRE: New Hampshire residents pay less in state taxes, per capita, than residents of any other state ($210.77 in fiscal year 1975). Delawarians, by contrast, pay $580.99 apiece in state taxes.

NEW ENGLAND'S COUNTIES

New England's Biggest County. AROOSTOOK, ME.: Aroostook County covers 6,821 square miles in northernmost Maine—most of it woods, bogs and potato fields. The states of Connecticut and Rhode Island would fit handily into Aroostook, with room left over for Washington, D.C.

New England's Smallest County. BRISTOL, R.I.: Bristol County's area is only 25 square miles.

America's Only State Bordered by a Single State. MAINE: New Hampshire is the only state touching a Maine border. Every other state has either no adjoining states (Alaska and Hawaii), or two or more.

Nation's Only Official State Spice. CONNECTICUT: Nutmeg is the official spice of Connecticut, the Nutmeg State. The spice was chosen to honor the memory of the traditional Yankee peddler, one of whose tricks was to sell fake nutmegs fashioned from bits of wood.

Nation's Only State Ladybug. FRANKLIN, MASS.: A second grade class in this town successfully proposed to the state legislature that the ladybug be made State Insect of the Commonwealth of Massachusetts. Most common ladybug in the state is the Two-Spotted Lady Beetle (*Adalia bipunctata*): head black with pale yellowish margin, elytra reddish with two black spots. Massachusetts co-opted the insect in Chapter 121 of the Acts of 1974. The way the children convinced the lawmakers to go through with their choice was to dress up as ladybugs on a visit to the capitol building.

Nation's Only State Praying Mantis. HARTFORD, CONN.: The Connecticut legislature here voted in 1977 to make the praying mantis the official State Insect.

Longest State Name. RHODE ISLAND: The smallest state has the biggest (official) name: State of Rhode Island and Providence Plantations.

State with the Fewest Poor. CONNECTICUT: Connecticut has fewer persons with incomes below the poverty level, as a percentage of the state's population, than any other state: 7.2% of Connecticut's people are below poverty level (compare 11.1% in California and 35.4% in Mississippi).

NEW ENGLAND'S WEALTH

New England's Most Prosperous Area. FAIRFIELD COUNTY, CONN.: The per capita annual income in Fairfield County is $4,646—the highest by far in New England, and one of the few highest in the U.S.

New England's Poorest Area. AROOSTOOK COUNTY, ME.: Aroostook County's per capita income is $2,053 per year, making Aroostook one of the poorest counties in the northern U.S.

America's Lowest Legal Marriage Age. MASSACHU-SETTS: Females aged 12 may marry in Massachusetts with parental consent; males must be 14 or more.

America's Only State To Have Five Capitals at the Same Time. RHODE ISLAND: Until 1854 Providence, East Greenwich, Bristol, Newport and South Kingstown were all state capitals. The General Assembly traveled from one to another to conduct its business. In 1854 the capitals were reduced to two, Newport and Providence, and in 1900 Providence was made sole capital.

America's First 18-Year-Old Majority. VERMONT: The state legislature admitted 18-year-olds to full adult privileges in 1971, before the rest of the nation followed suit (Amendment XXVI to the Constitution).

World's Only Suggested Tax on Sexual Intercourse. RHODE ISLAND: In December 1976 State Representative Bernard C. Gladstone suggested a $2.00 tax on sexual intercourse to replace the state income tax. The new levy was not approved.

NEW ENGLAND'S MIDDLES

The **Geographical Centers of the Six New England States** are located as follows:
  CONNECTICUT: East Berlin
  MAINE: 18 miles north of Dover
  MASSACHUSETTS: northern sections of Worcester
  NEW HAMPSHIRE: 3 miles east of Ashland
  RHODE ISLAND: 1 mile southwest of Crompton
  VERMONT: 3 miles east of Roxbury
The *approximate* geographic **Center of New England** itself is on the Maine–New Hampshire border, between Chatham, N.H. and North Fryeburg, Me.

Structures

World's Heaviest Birdbath (unofficial). MERIDEN, N.H.: The Helen Woodruff Smith Sanctuary here has a birdbath fashioned out of a five-ton boulder.

World's Largest Lobster Boiler. ROCKLAND, ME.: The Rockland Boiler is 24 feet long and has two 1,000-gallon tanks that can cook 5,000 pounds of lobster per hour. It is fired by a gas furnace developing two million BTUs.

World's Only *Spirit of St. Louis* Crate House. CONTOO-COOK, N.H.: The crate in which Charles A. Lindbergh's historic airplane was returned to the U.S. after his 1927 transatlantic flight now serves as a small home near Contoo-cook, according to a United Press report. A recent attempt to auction the crate off on the 50th anniversary of Lindbergh's flight brought no bidders.

World's Largest Unburied Time Capsule. WICKFORD, R.I.: Dr. Charles E. Daniel, a teacher of history at the University of Rhode Island, has had a six-foot-tall time capsule in his living room since July 1974. He and his wife, Violet, a high school history teacher, collected castings of commemorative coins, films of parades, newspaper clippings and programs from tricentennial events held during the 300th anniversary of Wickford. The Daniels had placed the material in their capsule, when it was discovered there was no place available to bury it. A sum of $8,000 put in escrow for land purchase of a two-acre site for the capsule from Penn Central railroad has still not been spent because of the bankruptcy of the firm.

Nation's Second Largest Monolithic Columns. PROVIDENCE, R.I.: The columns in the Westminster Arcade, installed in 1828, are exceeded in size only by those of the Cathedral of St. John the Divine in New York City. According to a report, "The huge columns were hauled into Providence by 15 yoke of oxen from the granite quarry at Bear Ledge in Johnston, R.I., on carts specially built." Each column weighs 13 tons. The columns are Ionic but not fluted, and cost $140,000.

World's Second-Largest Unsupported Dome. PROVIDENCE, R.I.: The 50-foot-diameter dome of the Rhode Island Statehouse has murals depicting Roger Williams colonizing Providence and a translation from Tacitus reading "Rare felicity of the times when it is permitted to think as you like and to say what you think." The dome, exceeded in size only by that of St. Peters, Rome, rises 235 feet above the terrace below. The Statehouse was built between 1895 and 1901.

World's Largest Circular Tank.   BOSTON, MASS.: The 200,-
000-gallon ocean tank of the New England Aquarium here is 23
feet deep and 40 feet in diameter. It contains 2,000 fish, including sharks and electric eels.

Nation's First Forest Fire Lookout Post.   GREENVILLE,
ME.: The M. G. Shaw Lumber Co. of Greenville put up a
"tower"—a log cabin with a flat roof—on Squaw Mountain
southwest of Moosehead Lake in 1905. The first watchman was
William Hilton of Bangor.

**America's Only Outdoor Reconstruction of Bethlehem and
Jerusalem.**   WATERBURY, CONN.: "Holy Land—U.S.A.,"
a miniature reproduction of the two holy towns, comprises
nearly 200 model buildings at Pine Hill here. Waterbury's
Bethlehem and Jerusalem are lighted at night by a great electric
cross.

World's Only Honorary Trysting Bench.   WESTERLY, R.I.:
The Gladys Ormphby Trysting Bench honors Ruth Buzzi of the
television program *Laugh-In,* who is a native of Westerly. It is on
the lawn of the Westerly Library.

Telecommunications

Nation's First Commercial Telephone Exchange. NEW HAVEN, CONN.: George Willard Coy was the first operator of the New Haven exchange, which began operations on January 28, 1878 servicing 21 subscribers. "Ahoy-ahoy," the operator shouted in answering the 'phone.

Nation's First News Dispatch by Telephone. BOSTON, MASS.: A call was put in from Salem, Mass., to the *Boston Globe* on February 12, 1877. The call itself constituted the news. The *Globe* reported, after receiving the call: "This special dispatch to the *Globe* has been transmitted by telephone in the presence of twenty people who have thus been witnesses to a feat never before attempted—the sending of news over the space of 16 miles by the human voice."

World's First Intelligible Telephone Message. BOSTON, MASS.: Alexander Graham Bell spoke the words "Come here, Watson, I want you" into a telephone on March 10, 1876, and was heard through the experimental device by Thomas Augustus Watson on another floor of Bell's home at 5 Exeter Place. That same year, on October 9, the two men held the world's first telephone conversation over outdoor wires when Bell, in Boston, spoke to Watson, two miles away in Cambridge. Parallel accounts of the conversations were published in the *Boston Advertiser* in answer to skeptics.

World's First Pay Telephone. HARTFORD, CONN.: The pay 'phone was invented here in 1889. The first one was installed in the Hartford Bank the same year.

World's First Home Telephone. SOMERVILLE, MASS.: Charles Williams, Jr., installed the first telephone for private home use in his house here in 1877.

Nation's First Long Distance Telephone Call. BOSTON, MASS.: Branch managers of the American Bell Telephone Company in Boston and New York spoke with each other over the telephone on March 27, 1884. The Boston *Journal* reported: "The words were heard as perfectly as though the speakers were standing close by, while no extra effort was needed at the other end of the line to accomplish the result."

Nation's Shortest Average Telephone Conversation. RHODE ISLAND: Bell Telephone reports that the average 3-minute, 54-second conversation in Rhode Island is the nation's shortest. Vermont's average is also under four minutes, while the other New England states are all over four minutes. The nation's longest average conversation, at 5 minutes, 43 seconds, is reported from Texas.

World's First Telephone Directory. NEW HAVEN, CONN.: The first phone book, containing about 50 names, was put out by the New Haven District Telephone Company in February 1878.

World's First International Telephone Call. CALAIS, ME.: The first telephone call to cross an international boundary was made here on July 1, 1881 between Calais and St. Stephen, New Brunswick, its neighbor across the St. Croix River.

World's First Telephone Saboteur (unofficial). BRATTLE-BORO, VT.: The world's first attempt to sabotage local telephone service was recorded from Brattleboro in 1877, the year the telephone came to the town. "Telephone poles . . . were being chopped down by an impetuous axman who did his mischief after nightfall," according to a recent account. The saboteur was exposed as a local attorney who felt the poles were unsightly.

World's First Semaphore Telegraph System. BOSTON, MASS.: Jonathan Grout of Belchertown, Mass., established a communications system between Boston and Martha's Vineyard in 1799 by building a series of towers, each one visible to a person atop the next, along the entire 90-mile distance. A combination of movements of flags and semaphores permitted the sending of messages, and Grout was able to ask a question from one end of the line of towers and receive an answer back from the other end within ten minutes.

World's First International TV Broadcast. ANDOVER, ME.: The first cross-ocean telecast was beamed from here on July 10, 1962, relayed from the Telstar communications satellite, and received at several European stations.

The Theater

World's Only International Opera House and Library. DERBY LINE, VT.: The Haskell Free Library and Opera House is the only institution of its kind in the world to be divided by an international boundary: the seats of the opera house are in Derby Line; the stage is in Rock Island, Quebec.

World's Only Play Scheduled To Coincide with the Full Moon. SWANZEY, N.H.: The nineteenth-century melodrama, *The Old Homestead,* is staged annually in a glade in the woods here as part of the Potash Bowl Festival in July, and because the moon plays a central part in the plot, the play goes on during three evenings when the moon is full. Most of the town's residents take parts in the production. The festival also includes church suppers and musical concerts.

America's First Summer Theater. SKOWHEGAN, ME.: The Lakewood Theater (now the State Theater) opened in 1901, presenting "popular summer fare," according to a report.

Nation's First Actor To Receive Applause at Curtain. BOS-
TON, MASS.: Edmund Kean, world-famous Shakespearean
actor, was given an ovation at the curtain in 1821 at a series of
performances at a Boston theater.

America's First Greek Play Produced in Greek. CAM-
BRIDGE, MASS.: Sophocles's *Oedipus Tyrannus* was played at
Harvard in May of 1881 with George Riddle in the title role.

Thoroughfares

World's Oldest Divided Highway. CARVER, MASS.: Savery's Avenue, half a mile long, was opened to traffic in 1861.

NEW ENGLAND'S TUNNELS

New England's Longest Tunnel. FLORIDA, MASS.: The Hoosac Tunnel, running about 4½ miles under the mountains between Florida and North Adams, is the longest railroad tunnel east of the Mississippi, and the fourth longest in the U.S. The tunnel was one of the engineering wonders of the world when it was finished in 1875 after about 22 years of work. Nitroglycerin explosive was first tested as a replacement for black powder in the blasting of the Hoosac Tunnel. Two million tons of rock were moved in building the tunnel, and twenty million bricks were used. Twelve trains of the Boston & Maine Railroad still pass through the Hoosac Tunnel each day.

159

America's Most Ambitious Road Sign. LYNCHVILLE, ME.: A sign outside town gives directions and distances to: Norway, Paris, Denmark, Naples, Sweden, Poland, Mexico, Peru and China—all of which are Maine villages within a couple of hours' drive of Lynchville.

World's Widest Sea-Level Canal. BOURNE, MASS.: The Cape Cod Canal runs 18 miles between Cape Cod Bay and Buzzards Bay. It is 500 feet wide—wider than the Panama and Erie canals. Planned in 1629, the Cape Cod Canal was one of the world's oldest uncompleted projects until its final construction between 1914 and 1919. The cruiser *Vacationer* takes summer visitors on a three-hour ride up and down the canal, sailing from the pier at Onset, Mass.

Tools

World's Biggest Nutcracker.   OLD LYME, CONN.: The implement hangs from a tree outside the Nut Museum here (*see under* Museums). The nutcracker is eight feet long.

World's First Crooked Scythe Snathes.   STERLING, MASS.: In 1828 Silas Lamson of Sterling patented the crooked scythe snathe, an innovation that greatly eased the work of mowers all over the world. Historically, the crooked snathe's dominance was short. It was only three years after Lamson's invention that the mechanical reaper of Cyrus McCormick (1831) began to put scythe snathes—crooked and straight alike—out of business for good.

America's First Cold-Cut Nails.   CUMBERLAND, R.I.: Jeremiah Wilkinson manufactured them, beginning in 1777. The nails were cut out of sheet iron (giving them a square section) rather than forged—a great savings of time and effort.

America's First Manufactured Sandpaper. SPRINGFIELD,
VT.: Patents on machinery which produced sandpaper were issued to Isaac Fisher, Jr., of Springfield, in 1834. Before Fisher's
inventions, people made their own sandpaper by gluing sand
onto scraps of paper, cloth or leather.

America's First Fork. BOSTON, MASS.: Governor John
Winthrop of the Massachusetts Bay Colony brought a fork to
the New World from England in 1630. Forks had been introduced in England by Queen Elizabeth "despite the flaming de-
nunciations of many clergymen."

World's Largest Frying Pan. PITTSFIELD, ME.: At the
Central Maine Egg Festival, held here on the last Saturday in
July, eggs are fried for 10,000 visitors in a frying pan 10½ feet
across, said to be the world's largest.

Trees

World's Only Rum and Water Elms. ALBION CORNER, ME.: Albion Corner's Rum and Water Elms are a relic of the great anti-liquor movement of the last century. They were planted in 1845. Local prohibitionists planted the trees on the south side of the street, anti-prohibitionists on the north. Whichever trees grew best would indicate which party Providence favored. Today the rum elms are bigger trees than the water elms.

Record-Setting Trees in New England

Hop Hornbeam. WINTHROP, ME.: A 78-foot-tall individual, the tallest in the U.S., growing near here was recorded in 1972.

Tamarack. JAY, ME.: A 95-foot specimen was recorded from here in 1972.

White Birch. HARTFORD, ME.: A 96-foot tree, the tallest in America, has been reported from Hartford.

White Pine. BLANCHARD, ME.: A specimen, thought to be the tallest in the U.S. at 147 feet, grows near here.

Vehicles

America's First Fire Engine. LYNN, MASS.: Joseph Jenks made a clumsy pump worked by men at handles for the selectmen of Boston in 1654. A bucket brigade supplied water to the pumper's cistern. Jenks was an ironmaker of Lynn.

America's First Steam Motorcycle. WINTHROP, MASS.: William A. Austin invented the machine in 1868. A steam boiler was suspended in the center of the cycle, which had a very limited traveling radius because of the small amount of steam it could generate.

World's Largest Tricycle. BOSTON, MASS.: Weighing over a ton, a tricycle was built in 1897 for the Woven-Hose and Rubber Co. here that had 11-foot wheels and could carry eight persons.

War

America's First Naval Battle. BLOCK ISLAND, R.I.: Near here in 1690 the veteran buccaneer Thomas Paine, with two boats, defeated a fleet of five vessels under the French privateer Captain Picard.

First Overt Act of the American Revolution. NEW CASTLE, N.H.: In December 1774 Major John Sullivan and a party of 400 volunteer militiamen attacked Fort William and Mary in New Castle. Major Sullivan's men, according to a report, "stole powder from the British here, which was later used against British at the Battle of Bunker Hill."

First Battle of the American Revolution. LEXINGTON, MASS.: At the scene of the first Revolutionary battle, the American John Parker encouraged his comrades in arms: "Stand your ground. Don't fire unless fired upon, but if they mean to have war let it begin here." The date was April 19, 1775.

America's First Naval Mine Barrage. NEW LONDON, CONN.: The inventor David Bushnell had the idea of using floating kegs full of explosives to blow up enemy ships. In August 1777 he attached a series of such mines together and floated them out into Black Point Bay for use against British warships in the area. The crew of the British frigate *Cerberus,* commanded by Captain J. Simmons, noticed a rope alongside and hauled it in, hoisting a mine aboard. The mine blew up, killing three men and knocking another overboard. Bushnell's mines had a gun lock with hammer set to explode on contact.

Northernmost Civil War Conflict. ST. ALBANS, VT.: On October 19, 1864, a band of Confederate raiders under Lieutenant Bennett H. Young struck St. Albans, robbed three local banks of a total of $200,000, and fled into Canada.

America's Only Town Shelled by a Submarine. ORLEANS, MASS.: In July 1918 a submarine bombarded a tug and three coal barges off Nauset Beach here. The U-boat—presumably German—fired a total of 147 shots and then submerged. A nearby airfield was alerted, but the flyers were all at a baseball game and none responded to the alarm until after the submarine had departed. The incident has never been satisfactorily explained.

Only State To Declare War on Germany Three Months Early in World War II. VERMONT: The state legislature declared "a state of belligerency with Germany" on September 11, 1941, almost three months before the Japanese attack on Pearl Harbor got the rest of the country into the war.

Nation's First Defense Blackout. LYNN, MASS.: On May 14, 1941 Lynn tested a blackout system in which all lights were turned out except for 12 "blackout luminaries"—2½-watt bulbs spaced at 100-foot intervals along Parkland Avenue. The bulbs produced ultraviolet rays that could not be detected from aircraft at 20,000 feet.

America's Only Hitler Hideout. GREENSBORO, VT.: There used to be a story in this town that Adolf Hitler was in hiding in the neighborhood of Caspian Lake, nearby. If he's still around, Hitler is 89 this year, making him one of the resort town's oldest residents.

Water

World's Largest Drinking Water Reservoir. AMHERST, MASS.: East of Town, Quabbin Reservoir covers 24,704 acres. Constructed in 1937, the reservoir inundated three local towns: Enfield, Greenwich and Prescott.

NEW ENGLAND'S LAKES

Biggest Lake in New England. GREENVILLE, ME.: Moosehead Lake, which lies to the north of Greenville, covers 117 square miles and has 190 miles of shoreline. Moosehead's maximum depth is 246 feet.

Second Biggest Lake in New England. LACONIA, N.H.: Lake Winnipesaukee, east of here, covers 70 square miles and is 169 feet deep at its deepest. Winnipesaukee has a longer shoreline than Moosehead's (240 miles).

World's Longest Lake Name. WEBSTER, MASS.: The Indian name of Lake Chargoggagonmanchaugagochaubunagungamaug means "You fish on your side of the lake; I fish on my side; nobody fishes in the middle."

America's Highest Tides. EASTPORT, ME.: The average rise of the tide at Eastport is 18 feet, 2 inches. The tides in this area—U.S. and Canadian waters of the Bay of Fundy—are the highest in the world.

NEW ENGLAND'S RIVERS

New England's Longest River. CONNECTICUT RIVER. The Connecticut, 407 miles long, rises in a system of small lakes near the Canadian border in New Hampshire, and enters Long Island Sound near Old Saybrook, Conn.

Second Longest River. ANDROSCOGGIN RIVER. The Androscoggin originates on the Maine–New Hampshire border and flows for 157 miles to join the Kennebec River (150 miles long—**New England's Third River**) near Bath, Me.

Weather

America's First Recorded Tornado.   NEW HAVEN, CONN.: A tornado struck New Haven in June 1682. This was the first tornado recorded for the country.

THE HURRICANE OF 'THIRTY-EIGHT

New England's Worst Catastrophe.   RHODE ISLAND: The Great New England Hurricane struck the northern shore of Long Island Sound on the afternoon of September 21, 1938 and tore across the region on a northwesterly course. Wind speeds exceeded 100 miles per hour on the coast, and 40-foot-high waves devastated the city of Providence and the beaches of Rhode Island and Massachusetts. At least 600 people died in the hurricane, and property damage in New England amounted to nearly $400 million.

World's Highest Recorded Wind Speed. MT. WASHING-
TON, N.H.: A speed of 231 miles per hour was recorded at the
summit of Mt. Washington (6,288 feet) on April 12, 1934. The
average wind velocity here is also the nation's highest: 35.2 miles
per hour, or a Force 7 blow ("Near Gale") on the Beaufort
Scale. P. T. Barnum once called Mt. Washington "the second
greatest show on earth."

Women

Nation's First Female Indian Fighter. HAVERHILL,
MASS.: Hannah Duston was captured by Indians from her
home in Haverhill on March 16, 1697. Duston and Mary Neff
were taken to an Indian camp where a Worcester boy, Samuel
Leonardson, was being held prisoner, having been captured two
years earlier. Duston killed ten of the Indians, scalped them,
and brought home the scalps as proof. She, along with Neff and
Leonardson, were all rewarded by the General Court of Massachusetts. Duston also received a pewter tankard from the governor of Maryland in recognition of her act.

America's First Woman Author. BOSTON, MASS.: Anne
Dudley Bradstreet, daughter of Governor Thomas Dudley and
wife of Governor Simon Bradstreet, in 1640 published a volume
of poems entitled: *Several Poems, compiled with great variety of Wit
and Learning, full of delight; wherein especially is contained a compleat
Discourse and Description of the Four Elements, Constitutions, Ages of
Man, and Seasons of the Year, together with an exact Epitome of the
Three first Monarchies, viz; the Assyrian, Persian and Grecian; and the*

beginning of the Roman Commonwealth to the end of their last King, with divers other pleasant and serious Poems; by a Gentlewoman of New England (unofficial holder of world's record for length of title in a book of poetry presenting an epitome of the three first monarchies).

America's First Woman to Make Writing a Profession. DEDHAM, MASS.: In 1784 Hannah Adams's first book appeared, an *Alphabetical Compendium of the Various Sects which Have Appeared from the Beginning of the Christian Era to the Present Day.* Her income from writing was very limited, according to a report.

Nation's Only City To Outlaw Lady Wrestlers. HAVER-HILL, MASS.: The city council bans female wrestling matches in Haverhill because "they undermine the dignity of womanhood."

America's First Countess. NORTH WOBURN, MASS.: Sarah Thompson's father, Benjamin Thompson, a North Woburn physicist, was made a Count of the Holy Roman Empire in 1791. In bestowing this noble title, Charles Philip Frederick, Duke of Bavaria, named daughter Sarah the Countess of Rumford. She had the privilege of living in any country in the world and had the right to half her father's pension.

Nation's First Woman Telephone Operator. NEWPORT, R.I. Kate Friend was hired by the Newport exchange in 1879, and worked as an operator there until 1894.

Largest Yo-Yo.   Cambridge, Mass.

Yo-Yo's

World's Largest Yo-yo.   CAMBRIDGE, MASS.: In 1973 students at the Massachusetts Institute of Technology dropped a 26-inch-diameter yo-yo from the roof of the 19-story Green Building. Reaching the end of its string, the yo-yo returned nine stories—to boos from spectators below. The yo-yo, which weighed 30 lbs., was constructed of a pair of bicycle wheels weighted with layers of steel strapping bolted around the rims. Two pie plates, painted with an anti-friction preparation, formed shields on the inner sides of the wheels, which were joined by an axle to take a wound cord of 400-pound-test braided nylon. The yo-yo was dropped from a nine-foot aluminum I-beam finger extending from the roof edge. The finger was equipped with a 1½-horsepower electric motor to give the cable a jerk when the wheel reached the bottom of its descent. Said Prof. Jim Williams, in charge of the project: "It was a success, because we created a concept and then brought it to reality."

Index